Glimpses

Glory

A Leaders Guide to Remembering Jesus at the Communion Table

Ron Kingham

Stonehaven Press
Oroville, CA
2013

You may contact the author through:
Stonehaven Press
70 Harry Lane
Oroville, CA 95966

ISBN 978-0-9898999-0-1

Dedication

This book is dedicated to the precious people of Woodland Bible Church in Woodland, CA. Your hunger to meet Jesus at His table became the impetus for my insatiable passion to reveal fresh memories each time we gathered there between 1978 and 2002. Many times during the preparation of this book I have seen your faces—your rapt attention, your awe and wonder, your tears of joy and repentance. Thank you for the many wonderful meals we shared together around our precious Savior's communion table. It is my prayer that the flame you ignited in me will kindle fires in many other places around this world through the message of this little book.

Acknowledgements

I am deeply grateful to friends and family who spurred me to write this book and then gave me invaluable counsel on shaping its message and tone. This long time pastor needed to acquire an author's voice. If it was accomplished, all credit goes to them. Special thanks go to Mike Myers, Arlene Hendriks, Mark and Bethany McKinley, Duane Davidson, and my beloved wife Cathy. Their eagle eyes and patient editorial guidance were a gift I can never repay.

Table of Contents

Chapter 1
Introduction

It's hard to live by faith in a sight-driven world. But if you're a follower of Jesus, that's exactly what you're called to do. What helps you keep your faith strong?

This book offers a tonic for faltering faith which comes straight from the Master Himself. It's been right in front of us for a very long time, but we were so familiar with it we may not have noticed it. It's time for us to take a good look at it. God's prescription for faltering faith is regular glimpses of Jesus' glory.[1] A person cannot get a true glimpse of the glory of Jesus and remain unchanged. A mere glimpse can shore up fading hope, bolster tottering faith, encourage the discouraged, reorient faulty priorities, cause the desires of the flesh to grow pale, and motivate the life of the spirit. When we are able to behold Him in the beauty of His matchless love and splendor, things of earth tend to fade into manageable perspective. When we are able to keep our eyes fixed on Jesus, we find strength to keep running the race of faith with endurance (Heb. 12:1-2).

Jesus wanted this for us. He expressed His deepest desires just before He died. He prayed,

> Father, I want those you have given me to be with me where I am, and to see my glory, the glory you have given me because you loved me before the creation of the world (John 17:24).

Of course, this was a future wish. He was longing for that day when there would be no more need for faith—for that day when we shall all be gathered to Him, and gaze on His face. But must we wait until faith is sight to see Jesus' glory? I don't think so. He established a place for us to snatch momentary glimpses of His glory right here and now. He intends for us to see and remember Him as we gather around His sacred communion table.

But for far too long, glimpses of Jesus' glory have been in short supply in many gatherings around the table. Too often, the observance of the Lord's table has become like salt which has lost its savor. Too many of God's leaders have allowed it to languish in the doldrums of the commonplace. We have failed to mine its Mother Lode of golden images of Jesus.

---

[1] For the purposes of this book, I define glory as "the outward and visible manifestations of one's inner qualities."

My Story

The message of this book is intensely entwined with my own personal story. It began in seminary—four years which remain a highlight of my life. I learned and grew by leaps and bounds in so many areas of my life and future ministry. I was stretched in the Biblical languages, theology, and countless other areas where I was equipped to preach God's Word and lead God's flock. I praise God for the professors who taught me, modeled Christ-like leadership, and motivated me to spend the rest of my days serving His people. I have only high marks for the ones who trained me and my cohorts.

At the same time, one of the glaring missing pieces of my training was any definitive theology of the Lord's table. I still remember the one day in Pastoral Care class in which we covered weddings, funerals, baptisms and the Lord's table all in one session! Looking back, I suspect that the reason the table drew such a short stick was that my mentors simply didn't believe it merited much more time. After all, how much training does it take to learn how to read Paul's words in 1 Cor. 11 and then pass out the little pieces of bread and the cup? They were training me, I suspect, to operate neatly within what I now call "the old model." A tacit agreement among church leaders was in place at that time, assuming the table was something to do regularly and reverently, but it didn't merit too much of our time and energy. The bulk of our pastoral vigor was to be devoted to the more important matters of the ministry. I don't recall anyone ever saying he/she prepared for the Lord's table like they did for other teaching events. What was there to prepare? But somehow I sensed there was more.

Following seminary I entered the pastoral ministry, and I continued the diligent study of God's Word. Little by little, I began to get a grasp of the matters in this book. Like the morning dawn, the table started to loom with increasing prominence in my personal construct of values and time allotments. I discovered that the table was—by far—the most effective tool I had for teaching my flock about Jesus. I couldn't afford *not* to give it top priority in my ministry. It would no longer get the short stick.

I made a solemn commitment to our Lord to give the table a very special place in my personal priorities of time, energy, and study. I pledged to devote some of my best creative and exegetical energy to the preparation and carrying out of communion services. I remember (somewhat audaciously, I think) challenging God to always give me a fresh look at the table. He took me up on that challenge. In the twenty four years I brought my flock before Jesus at His table, I always had a fresh topic. In fact, my files are still full of new ideas I have not yet pursued. This wonderful experience of watching the Holy

Spirit continually bring a fresh face to the teaching around the table only served to act as a divine imprimatur upon my thesis of its vital importance. Thirty five years later, I am absolutely convinced that this message needs to reach the hearts of those who lead God's flock to pasture.

I have written this book to challenge you to follow the rather unfamiliar trail I have attempted to blaze. I'm asking you to adopt a new model, to consider raising the table to a place of high priority and prominence in your teaching ministry. Seek to increase your flock's love for Jesus through its divinely designed memory-making methods, especially its multisensory appeal. I believe once you have experienced a few favorable responses from your flock, you will be sold. This approach to the table will become your passion, as it has become mine.

Cooking with Wok Chi

My wife and I have a favorite Chinese restaurant in our town. Not long ago I discovered one of the reasons the food is always so good: the owner and chef, Brian Wong, attempts to cook with a lot of *wok chi*. Says Wong, "Two chefs cooking the same dishes with the same ingredients, could be great or poor by possessing *wok chi* in the food or not!" He explains that

> *wok chi* is the ability of food to invoke a strong positive sensual response. It is done collectively through our sense of sight, smell, taste, and touch. With this in mind, we try to stir fry our food with the most *wok chi*. With the open kitchen, you can observe the chefs caramelizing sauces or searing the vegetables and meats under intense heat in their woks. The flames and crackles coming from inside the kitchen are our way of trying to achieve *wok chi* in our food.[2]

Do you put *wok chi* into your presentation of the Lord's table? I pray you will want to. Let's heat up the wok! The people are hungry.

This book is a call to restore the Lord's table to its rightful place in the worship and teaching of the church. Beyond that, it is a challenge to understand the table's amazing design. At the Last Supper Jesus declared that the bread and cup were to be taken "for the purpose of remembering Me again and again" (*meaning of the Greek at 1 Cor. 11:24 -25*). Memory is the aspect of our mental functioning which defines us as sentient beings. The thesis of this book is that our Lord intentionally aimed His table directly at our memory

---

[2] Brian Wong, on placemat at Tong Fong Low Restaurant in Oroville, CA, 2010.

since it is the very essence of our mind and personality. By instructing us to "Do this in remembrance of Me," it's as though He were saying, "I crafted your minds within your mothers' wombs, and I designed your capacity for memory to connect with this table so that you can truly see Me when you gather here."

If you lead God's flock, you are charged with the solemn responsibility of feeding His sheep. This book challenges you to revitalize your corporate experience around the table by first understanding and then fulfilling its heaven-sent design.

More Than Theory

As I said, what I will be sharing in these pages has been hammered out and validated in my personal experience. I had the wonderful privilege of planting and then pastoring a church in northern California. In the beginning I was ministering to a young flock who didn't have much aggregate experience with "church." Most of them didn't realize that the communion service was commonly just tacked on to the regular worship service once a month. They didn't know that the Lord's table had become rote and dry in many local congregations. They were unaware that many pastors seldom read anything other than 1 Cor. 11 when they offer the elements. Their naiveté was a great blessing, because it provided me with fertile soil for the cultivation of my budding passion to enrich memories of Jesus at the table.

We would gather around the table every six or seven weeks and devote the vast majority of the entire service to the theme we were considering that day. On those Sundays, the table was my pulpit, and the elements were prominently spotlighted in front of me.

The responses of the people confirmed the value of my efforts:

> "I felt His smile of love and forgiveness today."
> "I came here discouraged; I'm going away with hope and joy!"
> "Wow! I saw Jesus at the table today."
> "I never realized how much He suffered for me."
> "I never understood why His blood was so important to my faith."
> "I'm so glad we didn't leave for the weekend; this was where I needed to be."

Frequently, tears of joy, healing, and repentance accompanied these heart-felt comments.

Now most preachers would join me in saying we'd love to receive feedback like this after every sermon. But we don't. Sometimes it seems my sermons just float out the doors of the sanctuary and bypass every ear in the room. This was seldom the case with communion services at our church. That's a huge clue that the positive responses were not attributable to me. I was the same preacher. What was different was the table. Properly observed, the table becomes a place where God anoints us with divine eye salve opening our eyes to see Jesus—much like the miracle that brought a glimpse of Jesus' true identity to the couple[3] walking home to Emmaus:

> When he was at the table with them, he took bread, gave thanks, broke it and began to give it to them. Then their eyes were opened and they recognized him, and he disappeared from their sight. They asked each other, "Were not our hearts burning within us while he talked with us on the road and opened the Scriptures to us?" (Luke 24:30-32).

On one of those communion services in our church, participants might have had their senses heightened by any of the following:

• A blazing menorah lighting up the otherwise darkened room and illuminating the loaves of bread and cups of juice on the table. On that Sunday we were considering the way the lamp stand in the Old Testament Tabernacle was a marvelous picture of the One Who declared Himself to be the Light of our World.

• The bitter taste of parsley during a communion gathering which was also an enactment of the Passover. Bitter herbs powerfully portray the bitterness of sin's bondage. They set the stage for the joyful news that Jesus,

---

[3] Luke 24:13 and Mark 16:12 simply mention two *people*. Neither specifically states that they were husband and wife. However, many scholars equate the Cleopas in Luke with Clopas in John 19:25 for these reasons: Cleopas is the Greek version of the Semitic name Clopas. This is consistent with the fact that John's gospel reflects a more Jewish background, whereas Luke's is quite Hellenistic. There are many examples of Bible characters with multi-national names (e.g. Peter, Cephas, Simon; Paul, Saul; Silvanus, Silas; etc.). The narrative of Luke 24 includes details quite consistent with a husband and wife. For example they invited Jesus to "Stay with us" [i.e. in our home]. And they were personally acquainted with the women who had witnessed the empty tomb (Luke 24:22-24). This correlates well with John's account that one of the Marys who witnessed the crucifixion was the wife of Clopas. Some translations render *Ō anoētai* in Luke 24:25 as "O foolish *men*." However, it is literally "O foolish *ones*." See Gal. 3:1 where the same expression describes the whole congregation in Galatia, males and females.

like the Passover lamb of old, poured out His blood to redeem us from that bondage.

•The shrill blasts of a 3' long shofar (ram's horn trumpet) calling the folks to a communion service focused upon the meaning of the Feast of Trumpets and how it points to the great return of Christ someday soon.

•The piercing ring of a hammer driving nails into Jesus coming from behind the stage at the precise moment when a scripture was read about the crucifixion and a picture was displayed on the screen.

•The feeling of bare feet against the cold floor giving them firsthand experience of what it means to take off their shoes on holy ground.

•The surreal photo of an actual macrophage (a specialized blood cell that vacuums up foreign bacteria in the blood stream). On that Sunday we were examining how our physical blood is a beautiful illustration of what Christ's spiritual blood does to continually cleanse us from all sin (1 John 1:7). We also illustrated this principle at another communion service by blocking the cleansing flow of blood to a volunteer's arm with a blood pressure cuff. After a few moments, the volunteer's arm began to throb with increasing pain.

•An authentic photo of a stone olive press portraying the significance of the name Gethsemane (olive press), for it was in the garden called Olive Press that Jesus was crushed under the weight of the sin of the whole world.

Of course, these sensory images never stood alone. They were always enhancing the auditory expositional teaching of the scriptures. They were designed to cultivate a synesthetic picture of Jesus and to sharpen previous remembrances of Jesus, and they were always set in the context of the bread and cup spotlighted in the center of the room.

I challenge you to join me in investing your best exegetical and creative energy into your observances of the Lord's table. To do this with passion and credibility, you need to be equipped with a fuller understanding of what Jesus meant when He said, "Do this in remembrance of Me." This is what we will be probing in the coming chapters. Before we do, however, let's examine how the Lord's table came to lose much of its savor in recent years.

* * * * *

Chapter 2
Etiology of a Casualty

Take Inventory

Let's get honest for a minute. Give yourself a grade for the quality of your experience at the Lord's table—whether you or someone else was leading. Is it a vital time of deep spiritual connection with God? Do the people look forward to it with passionate eagerness? Is it fresh and rich with new meaning each time you gather there? Does it impact the senses in such a way as to bring sweet glimpses of Jesus?

Or has it lost its luster? Do you find yourself less than enthusiastic as you anticipate its coming? Is it akin to the way you feel when Christmas rolls around and you realize the story hasn't changed from last year?

I remember an occasion when I was fishing for trout in the Sierra Nevada mountains of California. Trout can be very fickle in their bait of choice, and when you finally discover what they want, you don't want to run out. On this particular day they were crazy about hellgrammites (ugly little black larva about an inch long that live under rocks in the shallow water along the shore of the lake). The fish were biting, but I was spending most of my time hunting under rocks for more hellgrammites. Every time I found a hellgrammite it meant another fish. I'll never forget the moment when I spied another hellgrammite—at least I thought it was one. It looked just like a hellgrammite, but when I grabbed it, it was only an empty exoskeleton. The adult dobsonfly had escaped, and what was left behind was just an empty form. It looked just like a hellgrammite, but it was *completely devoid of life*.

Sometime back, my wife and I visited a large church which observes the table every Sunday. We went there specifically to experience the communion because one of the members had told us that "communion is always very meaningful at our church." In actuality, the communion itself took about 7 minutes and was almost completely disconnected from the rest of the service. My guess was that few of the people really *saw* Jesus during that brief period of time. This incident underscored the shallowness and superficiality which have become commonplace in the communion experience of so many believers today. We have come to know and accept an observance of the Lord's table that is mostly a dead hellgrammite.

Honestly evaluate your experience with communion: Has it become an empty shell from which much or all of the life has escaped? Are you going through the motions, saying the scripture, eating the bread, drinking the cup, but you're not really sure you're accomplishing anything eternal?

Why has this happened? Let's examine three particularly suggestive reasons in explaining how we got here.

Mass vs. Sermon

The first reason is what I call *historical-polemical*. Evangelicalism today is the great-grandchild of the protestant Reformation of the 15th and 16th centuries in Europe. Reformers like Wycliffe, Luther, Calvin, and Zwingli led a sweeping movement that rose up against the theological errors and moral corruption of the Roman Catholic church of the middle ages. There were many strands to their dissent, all of which focused around a return to the Bible and away from unBiblical traditions of popes and church councils which had dominated the powerful rise of Romanism. *Sola scriptura!* (scripture only!) was their familiar battle cry.

By the time of the Reformation, Roman Catholic Sunday meetings had become sacramental, i.e. a vehicle through which the church dispensed God's grace to the people. They were extremely liturgical and almost exclusively conducted in Latin not understood by most of the common people. The services, which were typically celebrated in huge cathedrals,[4] had become known as the mass, and were largely focused around the Eucharist. There might be some music and a very short sermon (or homily), but the bulk of the service was comprised of the priest sacrificing the blood and body of Jesus on the elaborate altar in the front of the room and then giving only the bread to the communicants in attendance. Because the doctrine of transubstantiation[5] had become canon law by this time, the administration of the bread (or host) was very carefully controlled so as to not cause sacrilege with the actual body of Jesus. The priest administered the host directly to the mouth so that the worshippers' hands made no contact with it, and the papally-appointed priests retained the exclusive right to drink the wine and officiate at the mass. Attendees could only watch the priest drink the cup.

---

[4] The word *cathedral* comes from the Latin meaning *place of the chair*, and was so used because Catholic church buildings were designed for the reigning bishop or pope to be seated on his throne in a prominent place in the front of the structure.

[5] Transubstantiation (still held by Roman Catholics) teaches that when the priest offers the bread and cup and then consecrates it, it actually becomes the very blood and body of Christ.

In many ways the mass had become synonymous with the doctrines and practices of Roman Catholicism. It is not surprising then that the mass became a serious target for the leaders of the Reformation. To them, it was an ostentatious display of obviously unBiblical theological errors. For example, they asserted that grace was not dispensed by the church through sacramental channels; rather, it was given freely by God to all who simply exercised faith in Christ (Eph. 2:8-9). It was *sola fide!* (faith only!). Scripture clearly stated that Jesus couldn't be sacrificed again and again at the altar. His sacrifice had been accomplished once for all at the cross (Heb. 7:27, 9:12,10:10). Paul's letter to the Corinthians commanded all who observe the Lord's table to eat the bread *and* drink the cup. Thus to exclude participants from the cup was wrong (1 Cor. 11:23-29). To most of the reformers, the doctrine of transubstantiation was also wrong. The bread and wine couldn't *become* the very body and blood of Christ. Of course, they argued significantly about what Jesus *did* mean when He said "This is My body" and "This is My blood," but they consistently agreed that it did *not* mean transubstantiation.[6]

The debate (war, really) between the reformers and the Roman Church over the Lord's table cut right to the core of the meaning of the Christian gospel. Thus, during the days of the Reformation, how one observed communion became a public badge displaying where one stood on the gospel. Those who courageously rose up against the abuses and errors of the Roman church were *excommunicated* (lit. sent out from communion), i.e. formally and publicly excluded from being able to receive grace from its sacraments. Excommunication was, in the dogma of Catholicism, a sentence of eternal damnation, and often it meant woeful persecution and even martyrdom.

In its desperate attempt to maintain control of ecclesiastical power, Rome countered the spread of the Reformation with what has been dubbed "The Inquisition." Roman authorities sought out suspected defectors and "inquired" into their beliefs and practices.

---

[6] The present book is premised upon the Zwinglian view, also called "the memorial view." It holds that what Jesus meant by "This is My body" and "This is My blood" was similar to what we mean when we hold up a photograph and say "This is my family." The photograph is a symbol which powerfully and accurately reminds us of the family, but the photograph is not the family. The Zwinglian view draws its primary support from the words of Jesus: "Do this in remembrance of Me." Scores of theological treatises have been written which debate the Catholic, Lutheran, Calvinistic, and Zwinglian views. The reader is referred elsewhere for that discussion. I recommend Andrew Paris' excellent treatment in *What the Bible Says About the Lord's Supper*, Joplin, MO: College Press Publishing Co., 1986.

The classic *Foxe's Book of Martyrs* relates many accounts of courageous men and women whose anti-Roman stand on the Lord's table cost them their earthly lives. One example of a courageous reformer in Venice, Italy, in 1547, was Francis Spinola:

> Francis Spinola, a Protestant gentleman of very great learning, being apprehended by order of the inquisitors, was carried before their tribunal. A treatise on the Lord's Supper was then put into his hands and he was asked if he knew the author of it. To which he replied, "I confess myself to be the author of it, and at the same time solemnly affirm, that there is not a line in it but what is authorized by, and consonant to, the holy Scriptures." On this confession he was committed close [i.e. secluded] prisoner to a dungeon for several days.
>
> Being brought to a second examination, he charged the pope's legate, and the inquisitors, with being merciless barbarians, and then represented the superstitions and idolatries practised by the Church of Rome in so glaring a light, that not being able to refute his arguments, they sent him back to his dungeon, to make him repent of what he had said.
>
> On his third examination, they asked him if he would recant his error. To which he answered that the doctrines he maintained were not erroneous, being purely the same as those which Christ and his apostles had taught, and which were handed down to us in the sacred writings. The inquisitors then sentenced him to be drowned, which was executed in the [following] manner....
>
> [A]s soon as sentence was passed, the prisoner had an iron chain which ran through a great stone fastened to his body. He was then laid flat upon a plank, with his face upwards, and rowed between two boats to a certain distance at sea, when the two boats separated, and he was sunk to the bottom by the weight of the stone.[7]

Passion for repudiating the Roman Catholic way of observing the Lord's table was a central theme of the writings of the great reformers. Many were burned at the stake clutching and reading from similar treatises as the one written by Spinola.

---

[7] John Foxe, *Foxe's Book of Martyrs*, Electronic Edition STEP Files Copyright 1999, Parsons Technology, Chapter VI, "An Account of the Persecutions in Venice."

Now, although the reformers didn't overtly seek to diminish the significance or centrality of the Lord's table in their reaction against the Roman abuses and errors, their struggles to restore the church to Biblicity did inevitably bring about a subtle but substantive shift in its place in the worship of the evangelical church. In reflecting upon this change, noted church historian, Phillip Schaff, observes,

> Here lies a cardinal difference between the Catholic and Evangelical cultus: in the former the sacrifice of the mass, in the latter the sermon is the center.[8]

In their passion to restore the preaching of the Word to its earlier exalted place in the apostolic tradition, the Lord's supper was inevitably forced off center stage. The spotlight of worship in the evangelical church growing out of the Reformation was now upon the preacher, the pulpit, the scriptures and the sermon. Protestant churches were no longer built as cathedrals with an altar; they were now constructed to draw attention to the pulpit and the preaching which emanated from it. Worship services were no longer centered around the mass but around the message. In fact, many protestant traditions began to observe the Lord's table only once a month or even once a year. Those groups which observed it more often did not tend to center their services around it. More and more it became a periodic activity which was seen as ancillary to the methodical weekly preaching of the scriptures. Certain protestant traditions such as the Plymouth Brethren and others provided notable exceptions to this movement away from the centrality of the Lord's table, but the verdict of church history is clear in showing us that the Reformation reallocated the evangelical focus away from the Lord's table and onto the sermon.

This shift was not an intentional swipe at the Lord's table meant to diminish its theological importance or denigrate its relevance in the life of believers. It was more the unintended collateral damage resulting from a painfully-fought war against Catholic abuses and errors. Just like the innocent victims of war, the Lord's table did not deserve to suffer such harm. Whether we like it or not, we are forced to face the sad reality that it did without doubt suffer.

---

[8] Phillip Schaff, *History of the Christian Church*, Electronic Edition STEP Files, Copyright 1999, Findex.com, Inc., Chapter 7, §97

In the rush to restore the church to Biblicity, the pendulum swung a little too far. In throwing out the dirty bathwater, we allowed the baby to suffer serious harm.

In a little book on communion, a veteran American pastor of a generation ago laments the way this post-Reformation shift had impacted the churches of his denomination bringing widespread disinterest in the Lord's table:

> [T]he observance of the Lord's Supper usually comes at the end of a regular, and sometimes all too long, preaching service, and this greatly minimizes its importance. Few have the fortitude to remain for what they have been taught to feel is rather a perfunctory service of inconsequential value. This is especially true when they have already had an hour and a quarter in Sunday school and probably as much in the church service. [9]

Many other commentators have made similar observations. For example, with a tinge of sarcasm, Marlin Jeschke suggests that the theological debates are less relevant than many of the modern empty observances of the table which have lost their vitality:

> High-church theologians love to talk about "real presence" in the Eucharist. Shouldn't we start talking about a "real supper," a "real table ... .. real eating" ("real food for real people")? Then maybe we could experience "real communion…."[10]

In the published report of a significant gathering in Ashland, Ohio, in 1994 of theologians and church leaders from many strands of the Believers' Church tradition, one of their very significant resolutions regarding the Lord's table was, "To be more creative in our efforts to make the communion service meaningful. Although constant experimentation would be unsettling, we should not be too set in the way we have always done things."[11]

Clearly, the hard fought battles of the reformation have indeed left their mark upon our modern observance of the Lord's table.

---

[9] Monroe E. Dodd, *Christ's Memorial,* Nashville: The Sunday School Board of the Southern Baptist Convention, 1934, p. viii

[10] Marlin Jeschke, "Making the Lord's Supper Meaningful" in Dale R. Stoffer, ed., *Lord's Supper: Believers Church Perspectives,* Scottdale, PA: Herald Press, 1997, p. 151

[11] Dale R. Stoffer, ed., *Lord's Supper: Believers Church Perspectives,* Scottdale, PA: Herald Press, 1997, p. 287

Stale Bread

A second reason for the dead hellgrammites is that familiarity and repetition have bred apathy and disinterest among those who lead at the table as well as those who eat there. The bread at the table has grown stale.

This is the nature of anything done repeatedly: without vigilant effort to keep it vital, it quickly loses its freshness and mystery. Like Pavlov's dogs, when our people show up at the table, and everything looks just like it always has, and everything sounds just like it always has, they are conditioned to quietly tune out and totally miss what is happening. However, unlike Pavlov's famous salivating dogs, much communion observance today is really Pavlov's law in *reverse*—when the familiar communion bell rings, our people *lose* their appetite for the table.

The Lord's table provides a particularly demanding challenge for the pastor and church leader: How do we do the same thing over and over again without it becoming rote and stale? It seems far too many of us have simply not risen to that challenge.

I don't think my own experience is unique. In the church my family attended during my formative years, it was our custom to receive communion on the first Sunday of every month. There was a large attractive table on the floor level directly under the pulpit prominently displaying the engraved words "In Remembrance of Me." On most Sundays it was set with a huge open family Bible and fresh flowers, but on communion Sundays it was set with beautiful silver trays containing bits of broken cracker fragments and neatly stacked trays full of tiny cups of grape juice. This was the only clue indicating it was communion Sunday until the pastor finished his sermon (which never seemed to have anything to do with receiving the bread and the cup).

On the first Sunday of the month, instead of dismissing the congregation at the conclusion of his sermon, he would announce, "Today is communion Sunday." He would allow anyone who didn't want to stay for the extra fifteen minutes to be quietly dismissed and then call two of the elders or deacons to join him at the front.

The pastor would then offer a one to two minute meditation on the significance of Jesus' death, followed by a reading of the pertinent verses from 1 Cor. 11. After that he would call the ushers to pass out the bread. One of the elders would thank God for the bread, and we would all eat. The scenario would be repeated with the cup. As soon as the cup was emptied, he would say, "Jesus and his disciples sang a hymn as they left the Upper Room, so let's stand and sing a hymn as we're dismissed."

Now it is clear that the repeated observance of this very predictable communion service planted memories deep within my long-term memory. Fifty five years later, I am able to replay the scene as though it were yesterday. What is very sad to me is that despite so many times eating the bread, drinking the cup, and watching the experience play out before me, I cannot say that I often *remembered Jesus*. It was certainly not my common experience to see "glimpses of His glory" as we discussed in the Introduction. What was intended by God to be a very salty experience had lost much or all of its saltiness (Matt. 5:13).

I am reminded of the story recounted in Acts 6:1. The apostles were becoming overloaded with preaching, evangelizing, and praying, and they found it difficult to keep up with the practical needs of some of the members of their flock. Luke describes the problem this way: Some of the non-Jewish widows were being overlooked in the daily distribution of food. So they thoughtfully and prayerfully changed their methods to assure that the widows' needs could be properly addressed. As I look back on my early experience of the Lord's table—as well as the common experience of many congregations today—I think a parallel statement could be made: Many of the people's spiritual needs were—and are—being overlooked and neglected in the distribution of the bread and cup. Change is needed.

But far too few of us church leaders have been willing to pursue change. We have allowed the familiar to breed apathy and emptiness. We've been content to feed our flocks stale bread. We've allowed them to be overlooked in the distribution of the food.

I invite you to pray with me, "Enough stale bread! Lord, I want to lead my flock to good pasture. I want them to experience the richness and vitality of the Lord's table as You planned it. I want them to touch and smell and taste *fresh* bread and wine each time we gather together around the table. Lord, I hunger to lift their marveling eyes to snatch Emmaus-Road glimpses of Jesus at the table. I want them to receive the blessings You intended when You designed and instituted this glorious place to remember You."

Now if that prayer expresses the aspirations of your heart, the immediate follow-up question must be: What is the design crafted into the Lord's table which will bring it to life each and every time it is observed? This book sets out to answer that question. Unawareness of the grand design is the third reason why I believe so much modern evangelical communion practice has become a dead hellgrammite.

It Was There All the Time; I Just Didn't See it.

We do it often. We look right past the obvious and fail to see it. I think this has certainly been the case with our experience of the Lord's table. It's been there—right in front of our eyes—often engraved into the ornate wood of our communion tables: "Do this in remembrance of Me." We need to stop and notice what this means: The Lord's table is aimed directly at our human capacity to remember.

Why did God link the table to our human capacity to form memories? How do our memories work (and not work)? What is the relationship between the way our memories work and the input they receive from the various senses? How does the simple makeup of the table (being composed of eating bread and drinking wine or juice) lend itself powerfully to evoking vivid and unforgettable images of Jesus? These, and a host of other questions probe at the fundamental core of the design.

For far too long we evangelicals have postponed investigating these questions. We remain ignorant of the compelling multisensory design of the table. In searching the extensive Christian literature on the subject of communion, one is hard pressed to find anyone who has pursued this fundamental linkage between the multisensory design of the table and the way our memories work. Yet both the Old and New Testaments have a great deal to say about the importance and meaning of our memories. In addition, modern science—especially psychology and neuroscience—has probed deeply into understanding the complex mechanisms of our memories, lending remarkable insights which are incredibly pertinent to the table.

So the task before us is to explore the scriptures on the subject of memory and then to carefully weave the strands of Biblical and scientific knowledge together. In so doing, we can discover a practical plan which will capitalize upon the exquisite design of the communion table, enabling us to make the most of its full potential for leading our people to see fresh, life-changing glimpses of Jesus every time we gather there.

To summarize, we have observed three important reasons why much modern evangelical experience with the Lord's table receives fairly low marks in its ability to evoke Emmaus-Road glimpses of Jesus' glory: 1) the Reformation shift from the mass to the sermon, 2) dryness of familiar repetition, and 3) ignorance of the multisensory design of the table and its linkage to our human capacity to form memories. Let us note carefully that these low marks are not because of any problems with the nature of the table itself; rather, they are problems with the church's *experience* of the table. Like a football team which has an excellent game plan but then goes out and loses badly, the fault was not in the game plan but in the *execution* of the plan.

*   *   *   *   *

Chapter 3
The Pinnacle of Worship

Jesus taught us that the Heavenly Father seeks worshippers who will worship Him in spirit and in truth (John 4:24). To its credit, the American church has seriously sought to cultivate this kind of worship in recent years. We allot a significant amount of time every Sunday to "worship." However, usually when we speak of worship today, we are referring to the restricted aspect of *worship through music*. Yet a brief survey of the topic will show that worship is a much broader subject than mere music. It includes all types of activities and attitudes which enable us to show God how much we creatures adore our Creator and we redeemed ones revere our Redeemer.

Many of these worship activities spring from deep within us and reflect the kind of people we are. Forms of worship vary from culture to culture and from age group to age group. Worship unquestionably has many faces.

Without doubt, because of its magnificent design, the table should be one of the most significant and meaningful forms of worship celebrated in the life of any local church body. It should open the eyes of the congregation to see Jesus in ways not available to other paths of worship. What follows are eight of the extraordinary qualities of the Lord's table which set it apart as the pinnacle of worship.

1. Designed by God

In contrast to the many forms of worship that spring from human diversity, the Lord's table is not humanly conceived. It is not reflective of one particular culture or age group. Of course, its observance will rightly spring from the culture of its celebrants, but in its purity and simplicity as broken bread and wine received in remembrance of Jesus, it has no attachments to any person or people group. It was instead handed to us by the Creator/Redeemer Himself. The same One Who designed life on this planet and then skillfully crafted redemption through the blood of Jesus is the One Who designed the worship at the table. He passed the bread and the cup and then commanded, "You do this until I come back!" To remember Jesus is to worship Jesus.

How can a creature improve upon the work of his or her Creator? It is blasphemy to even entertain the notion! The Lord's table is just as marvelous a creation as a delicate spring wildflower or a newborn baby. In our modern day rush to be innovative in our worship, we must not overlook the magnificently conceived form of worship crafted by the Designer Himself. Since He designed the table, we can be sure it will be exquisitely effective in cultivating true worship in our people.

2. Elegantly Simple yet Eminently Profound

A simple meal. Broken bread and a cup of juice. Eaten and drunk to remember Jesus. Nothing complicated or arcane. Yet with these plain elements we are enabled to understand and personalize the meaning of the otherwise incomprehensible constellation of redemptive events surrounding the incarnation. This fact alone should stir up awe in our hearts as we gather on the holy ground around the table.

3. Universal

As noted above, the table cuts across all ethnic, cultural, geographic, and age-group boundaries. It is a worship form for all people in all ages. The elements are readily available almost anywhere (especially in this age of globalization). In those isolated regions of the earth where bread and grape juice or wine are not easily obtainable, substitutes can readily be found. The nature of the design as drama appealing to many senses is understandable by all, regardless of age, language, or culture.

4. Focused on Jesus

The Lord's table is not just *about* Jesus; it is a specially designed place where by faith we actually *see* Him both in His suffering and in His glory, as the humble servant and the King of Kings. Our daily experience as believers is the struggle to live for Jesus, to follow Jesus, to love and be loved by Jesus—all without actually seeing Him. Yet the writer of the epistle to the Hebrews exhorts us to run the race with our eyes fixed upon Jesus (12:1-2). It is a fight to keep walking by faith and not by sight, and so (like the couple who met Jesus on the Road to Emmaus) our faith is powerfully fortified whenever we are privileged to get an encouraging glimpse of the Savior. The table wonderfully transports us away from the distractions of this chaotic sight-oriented world and into the presence of the One Who is the author and finisher of faith.

Jesus is the worthy and rightful beneficiary of all our worship. Revelation 4 and 5 picture Him in His glory in heaven receiving the worship of the angelic multitudes because He is the Creator and Redeemer of the human race. It is a foretaste of what we will someday be doing when our faith has been transformed into blessed sight. What a privilege it is to have a table around which we can gather *now* and see Him by faith.

5. Aimed at the Memory

Our memory is so much a part of our daily lives we often fail to notice its astounding presence and power. Yet, it is one of the most vital traits we possess. To understand the importance of memory, all one has to do is observe the breakdown of memory in a person with a debilitating brain disorder such as Alzheimer's disease. Memory is central to our ability to think and learn and know. It is one of the characteristics which sets us apart as human beings made in the image and likeness of God.

In fact, our memory has been called the nexus of the human mind. The word nexus is derived from the Latin meaning *the binding or fastening core*. This is surely an apt word to describe our memory, for the data processing (believed to be largely centered in a portion of our brains called the hippocampus) is what enables us to see, think, speak, listen, write, and do all the other amazing things minds do. Scientists have studied patients who have had their hippocampus surgically removed and found them to be unable to function in society because every perception and momentary experience is constantly brand new without any context for evaluation.[12]

A well respected authority on memory, Dr. Elizabeth Loftus, has written:

> The human mind, holder of vast memories, is intricately constructed. As Cicero said in *De Oratore*, "Memory is the treasury and guardian of all things." Without memory, life would consist of momentary experiences that have little relation to each other. Without memory we could not communicate with one another—we would be incapable of remembering the thoughts we wished to express. Without memory, a person would not have the sense of continuity even to know who he or she was. Without a doubt, memory is central to being human.[13]

Dr. Eric Kandel, Nobel prize winner for his ground-breaking research into the way brain cells change when they store memories, says: "We are who we are because of what we learn and what we remember."[14]

---

[12] See for example the well documented case of "George M." in Philip J. Hilts, *Memory's Ghost*, NY: Simon & Schuster, 1995

[13] Elizabeth Loftus, *Memory*, Reading, MA: Addison-Wesley Pub. Co., 1980, p. 2

[14] Eric R. Kandel, *In Search of Memory*, New York: W. W. Norton & Company, 2006, p. 10

Because of its fundamental centrality to our humanity, a vast branch of psychology is devoted entirely to the study of memory. It is no accident, then, that our Lord aimed His table directly at our memory, for it is the very essence of our mind and personality.

6. Provides Opportunity to Engage All the Senses

I mentioned above that the experience of the couple who met Jesus on the Road to Emmaus is a model for us in what it means to get true glimpses of Jesus' glory. Luke reports that their hearts burned within them when they finally understood what He was saying, and they recognized they were actually looking into His face (Luke 24:30-35). This memory was powerful because it was created by a synesthetic experience of Jesus. The deepest reaches of their spirits and emotions were stirred because they had *seen* Him and *heard* Him and *touched* Him and *eaten* the bread and perhaps even *smelled* His familiar fragrance. In the same way, the Lord's table invites us to participate in a synesthetic experience of Jesus, to remember Him by engaging all the senses.

Memory experts describe the process of learning which takes place within our minds as the progression from *perception* to *conception*. Perception involves receiving the incoming information via the gates we call senses; conception involves processing the raw data of perception in order to find meaning in what we have perceived and understand it. All we know must come to us through our senses.

It is generally thought that memories are stored (for the long term) in bits and pieces encoded with retrieval tabs, handles somewhat akin to the way we file books in a library or data in a computer. Retrieval tabs are like the key words search engines use to locate information on the internet. The more retrieval tabs, the more accessible is the memory. In addition, the more varied the retrieval tabs, the more vivid is the memory. This is especially true when the memory has been encoded with handles from many of our senses. Hence we say that a synesthetic experience is very memorable.

Is it not, then, significant that Jesus would enrich His place of remembrance with many potential retrieval tabs for our senses? Charles Spurgeon spoke with insight on this point:

> Behold the whole mystery of the sacred Eucharist. The power to excite remembrance consists in the appeal made to the senses. Here the eye, the

hand, the mouth, find joyful work, and thus the senses, which are usually clogs to the soul, become wings to lift the mind in contemplation.[15]

Chapter five will explore this in more detail.

7. Involves Action

In his helpful book, *Preaching on the Lord's Supper*, Ian MacLeod points out a fascinating fact of Scottish church history:

> One of the names applied to the Lord's Supper in the early reformed Scottish Church was the "action." So it was described in Knox's Book of Common Order, and almost a century later, in the Westminster Directory for public worship, "the minister is to begin the *action*, with sanctifying and blessing the elements." Indeed, until comparatively recent times, the sermon preached immediately before the celebration of the sacrament was known as the "action sermon." That name has now fallen into disuse, but at least it had this to be said for it, that it preserved the present sense - the "this do now" of the sacrament, and also the sense of its being an acted sermon or an acted proclamation of the death of our Lord.[16]

The Lord's table is not a performance to be watched; it is an action to be done. Without doubt, there is much to see at the table, but as MacLeod notes, Jesus said to *do* this, not to just watch this. Surely there should be much to think about at the table, but He said, "*Eat* this bread and *drink* this cup," not "Think about bread and wine."

Learning experts have long pointed out that the path to learning things well—i.e. so that they can be easily and correctly remembered—must include some sort of *doing*. Memory experts explain that this occurs because our so-called "motor memory" is much less subject to decay than our cognitive memory. Here then is excellent educational technique built right into the table. Here is a place to encode deeply memorable pictures of Jesus.

---

[15] C.H. Spurgeon, in Joseph Exell, *The Biblical Illustrator*, @ 1 Cor. 11, Vol. II, Grand Rapids: Baker Book House (n.d.), p. 105

[16] Ian MacLeod, *Preaching on the Lord's Supper*, Peabody, MA: Hendrickson Publishers, 1990, p. 38-39. MacLeod's book also includes an excellent sermon on the connection of the five sense to the table.

8. Teaches with Analogies

Speaking of excellent educational technique…. I mentioned above the progression in cognitive learning from perception to conception. Psychologists describe the way our minds develop concepts as a process of evaluating, comparing, and contrasting new thoughts and percepts against already stored notions. This is especially effective when we compare and contrast ideas via analogy from the concrete to the abstract. Abstract ideas have no real existence in the time-space world. They only exist as notions within our mind. For example, one cannot find a specimen of loving redemption in the earth somewhere and examine it with the senses. One must observe concrete examples which exhibit similar traits.

The Old Testament is a storehouse of concrete redemptive analogies such as the sacrifice of innocent animals, the kinsman-redeemer, Noah's ark, the Tabernacle, etc. All of these are readily perceived by our senses. As we perceive these concrete analogies visually, audibly, and even by touch, taste and smell, we are able to understand the complex qualities of the abstract redemption provided by Jesus at the cross.

The table is ripe with opportunities to teach via analogy. Even the very elements themselves are emblems or symbols of very complex theological concepts barely understood by the most erudite Bible scholars. Yet, we *can* observe how the physical blood cleanses us from impurities within our bodies; we *can* experience how crushed and baked wheat nourishes us and sustains our physical lives, etc.

The table gloriously and uniquely links the powerfully pregnant concrete symbols of the natural world with the sublime abstract realities of the redemptive message of life in Christ. There is nothing else quite like it.

Again, the One Who designed our minds to learn via analogy also designed His table to teach us via analogy.

Restoring Balance

My prayer is for you to hunger to join me in another reformation—a reformation to restore vitality to the Lord's table. Instead of viewing the table as ancillary to the sermon or worship, we will see it as *essential* to excellent teaching and *vital* to genuine worship. We will give ourselves to understand its rich design appealing to our memories through the senses, and we will prayerfully invest our best energies in bringing it alive among our people. May it be restored to its rightful place in a balanced ministry right alongside the other activities that characterized the early apostolic church described in Acts 2:42: "They devoted themselves to the apostles' teaching and to the fellowship, to the breaking of bread and to prayer."

John Chrysostom was an eloquent preacher and careful expositor of the scriptures who ministered in ancient Antioch during the last half of the fourth century. He is well known for his fervent passion as a powerful speaker (his name means "golden mouth"). He also had a great love for the Lord's table. That dual passion is preserved in the symbol that has been used ever since to represent his life and ministry: the Bible and the chalice. I invite you to join me and Chrysostom in cultivating a dual passion for the accurate and powerful preaching of the Word *and* the vital observance of the Lord's Table.

Such passionate attention to the Lord's table begins with understanding what it means to "Do this in remembrance of Me." This is what we will examine in chapter four.

*   *   *   *   *

Chapter 4
In Remembrance of Me

Forgetting Christ

Spurgeon rather bluntly reminds us of a rueful plight plaguing all of us:

> Christians may forget Christ. It seems at first sight too gross a crime to lay at the door of converted men; but if startling to the ear, it is, alas! too apparent to the eye. Forget Him who never forgot us! Who loved us even to the death! The incessant round of world, world, world; the constant din of earth, earth, earth, takes away the soul from Christ. While memory will preserve a poisoned weed, it suffereth the Rose of Sharon to wither.... The cause is apparent. We forget Christ, because regenerate as we are, still corruption remains.[17]

Those who study the arrangement of our remarkable capacity for memory are quick to point out its frailties. In his book *The Seven Sins of Memory*,[18] Daniel Schacter documents a myriad of ways that we forget and/or bias our memories. Some of these findings are very pertinent to our study of the Lord's table, and they will help us in our quest for improving its observance.

Given our proclivity for forgetfulness, it is not surprising that the Old Testament teems with admonitions such as "remember your God" and "don't forget His law" and "remember how you were a slave in Egypt and God delivered you." God knows the weakness of our flesh (e.g. Psa. 103:14), and He knows that if we don't take proactive action to fight the tendency to forget, we will quickly lose access to essential truths. Take for example the strong admonition of Moses to the Israelites as they were about to enter the promised land:

> When the LORD your God brings you into the land he swore to your fathers, to Abraham, Isaac and Jacob, to give you—a land with large, flourishing cities you did not build, houses filled with all kinds of good things you did not provide, wells you did not dig, and vineyards and olive groves you did not plant—then when you eat and are satisfied, be careful that you do not forget the LORD, who brought you out of Egypt, out of the land of slavery (Deut. 6:10-12; see also Deut. 8:10-14).

---

[17] C. H. Spurgeon *in* Joseph Exell, *The Biblical Illustrator*, 1 Cor. Vol. II, Grand Rapids: Baker Book House (n.d.), p. 107

[18] Daniel L. Schacter, *The Seven Sins of Memory*, Boston: Houghton Mifflin Co, 2001

The New Testament is also amply supplied with commands to remember and exhortations to not forget (e.g. "Remember Lot's wife," Luke 17:32, "I want you to recall the words spoken in the past by the holy prophets and the command given by our Lord and Savior through your apostles," 2 Pet. 3:2). One New Testament word, *mnēmoneuō*, is particularly fitted to describing the way memories become dull and faded. Consider a couple of examples. *Mnēmoneuō* is used to describe the astonishing phenomenon of a woman quickly forgetting the excruciating pain of childbirth:

> A woman giving birth to a child has pain because her time has come; but when her baby is born she forgets [lit. *no longer remembers*] the anguish because of her joy that a child is born into the world (John 16:21).

Within hours of witnessing one of Jesus' greatest miracles—the feeding of more than five thousand people with one little boy's lunch—the disciples were discussing where they would find food to eat. Jesus admonished them for the rapid decay of their fading memories:

> ...You of little faith, why are you talking among yourselves about having no bread? Do you still not understand? Don't you remember the five loaves for the five thousand, and how many basketfuls you gathered? (Matt 16:8-9).

James also speaks of our penchant for forgetting quickly in James 1:23-24. This text employs another word, *epilanthanomai*, which means literally *to allow to become hidden from conscious view*:

> Anyone who listens to the word but does not do what it says is like someone who looks at his face in a mirror and, after looking at himself, goes away and immediately forgets what he looks like.

Since the Bible speaks so candidly of our tendency to forget quickly, we should not be surprised to learn that science also confirms this. Memory experts tell us one of the reasons we forget so much so quickly is the "central processing register" in our brains (probably centered in the region known as the hippocampus) receives way too much sensory input to handle. It must "triage" the tsunami of data constantly bombarding it, discard the vast majority as irrelevant, and process the little bit that our mind decides is important. Unfortunately, our darkened intellects often have a mind of their own, and wind up discarding the baby and storing the bathwater.

A classic study was done several decades ago by a psychologist named Ebbinghaus. He memorized long lists of basically nonsensical information and then tested his memory. He plotted the results (in what has become known as the "Curve of Ebbinghaus") and found that memory decays exponentially within minutes. If attention is not given to the matters learned, more than 50% is lost within the first twenty minutes, and another 10% is lost within an hour. In other words, after one hour a person only retains 40% of what was learned the hour before. The curve flattens out after this, with 25% of the original material being retained after five days. "[T]his function has stood the test of time, and has been shown to apply across a very wide range of material and learning conditions,"[19] comments Alan Baddeley, another noted memory expert. In other words, our memories are wide-mesh sieves.

Our own personal experience confirms this every day, and thus it is not hard for us to have compassion on the disciples for forgetting the miraculous bread. When Peter tells us he is reminding us of things we already know (2 Pet. 1:12), we accept his instruction because the things we "know" have too often grown a bit fuzzy.

A story used to circulate around the campus of the seminary I attended in Dallas, Texas. It concerned a much beloved "absentminded professor." It seems that Professor So-and-so had a weekend speaking engagement in Houston. So having kissed his wife good bye on Saturday, he traveled to the church. He ministered there, and then after the final meeting, he asked one of the church members to drive him to the airport. After purchasing a ticket, he flew home to the Dallas airport. From the airport he telephoned his wife, asking her to come and pick him up. "In what?" she responded. "You drove the car to Houston!"

Our memories are quite frail indeed, but the humor quickly evaporates when our affinity for forgetting affects the most important relationship in our lives. Listen again to the words of Spurgeon: "Christians may forget Christ." As he eloquently pointed out, in "the incessant round of world, world, world" and "the constant din of earth, earth, earth" our memories of our beloved Lord deteriorate and even disappear. Ancient Greek mythology blamed a person's forgetfulness on having been plunged into the River Lethe, the river of forgetfulness. But we who believe the scriptures need look no further than the ever-present traces of our fallen nature.

---

[19] Alan Baddeley, *Your Memory: A User's Guide*, NY: MacMillan Pub. Co., 1982, p. 49

With this thought as background, let us reconsider the words of Jesus as recorded by Paul in 1 Cor. 11.

> For I received from the Lord what I also passed on to you: The Lord Jesus, on the night he was betrayed, took bread, and when he had given thanks, he broke it and said, "This is my body, which is for you; do this in remembrance of me" (*eis tēn emēn anamnēsin*). In the same way, after supper he took the cup, saying, "This cup is the new covenant in my blood; do this, whenever you drink it, in remembrance of me." For whenever (*hosakis ean*) you eat this bread and drink this cup, you proclaim the Lord's death until he comes (1 Cor. 11:23-26).

The key phrase here, of course, is "Do this in remembrance of Me." But twice it adds "whenever you do this" (*hosakis ean*). The master grammarian, Robertson, says that this is the "[u]sual construction for general temporal clause of repetition (*an* and the present subjunctive with *hosakis*)."[20] In other words, Jesus is saying, "Remember Me *repeatedly*." Thus, not only is the Lord's table aimed at our memories, the very nexus of our minds (as we saw in the previous chapter), but in addition, here we see it also targeting our tendency to forget. We need to observe it over and over again in order to keep from forgetting Him and to correct and refine old memories that aren't perfectly accurate. Brain experts Sandra Aamodt and Sam Wang explain how this works:

> …one can locate an offending memory, play it back, then erase it like an unwanted computer file. Research in the past few years suggests that recollection of a memory also reinforces the memory. There is good evidence that we "erase" and "rewrite" our memories every time we recall them, suggesting that if it were ever possible to erase specific content, playing it back first might be an essential component.[21]

As Jesus gazed into the eyes of those disciples who were about to become the apostles who would spread the gospel all over the world, He lovingly anticipated their weakness (and ours!) and made a wonderful plan to combat it.

---

[20] A. T. Robertson, *Word Pictures in the New Testament, Vol. 4: Epistles of Paul*, Electronic Edition STEP Files Copyright © 1997, Parsons Technology, Inc., PO Box 100, Hiawatha, Iowa.

[21] Sandra Aamodt and Sam Wang, *Welcome to Your Brain*, New York: Bloomsbury, 2008, p.13

Remembering Christ—the Lexical Meaning of *Anamnēsis*

Now let's examine the word in 1 Cor. 11 that is at the heart of our exploration, *anamnēsis, remembrance*. It is part of a whole family of Greek words used in the New Testament to describe the multitude of ideas surrounding memory, cognates built around the root *mnē-*.[22] This large family of words with subtle shades of meaning points out just how important the notion of remembrance was at the time of the writing of the New Testament.

The suffix on this key word, *anamnēsis*, indicates *an action or activity*; and the prefix denotes *again*. Very literally it means "an activity that is repeated to summon a memory." The only other New Testament usage (outside the communion texts) well illustrates this notion. Heb. 10:3 describes Old Covenant sacrifices that were repeated year after year with the purpose of reminding God's people of sin:

> But those sacrifices are an annual reminder (*anamnēsis*) of sins.

So, from a purely lexical standpoint, by employing *anamnēsis* in the communion texts, Luke (22:19) and Paul (1 Cor. 11:24-25) were relating Jesus' plan to establish an activity that would be repeated over and over again to evoke remembrance of Himself. We are reminded of the stones of remembrance that Joshua placed in the Jordan River to be visited over and over again to constantly remind the Israelites and their children of their miraculous crossing at flood stage (Josh. 4:1-9). In contrast to those lifeless stones of remembrance, Jesus was calling us to "…come to him [at His table], the living Stone [of remembrance]—rejected by humans but chosen by God and precious to him" (1 Pet. 2:4).

Remembering Christ: Two Key Aspects—His Person and His Passion

Now as we examine the phrase "Do this in remembrance of Me" we see two key aspects of this remembrance—remembrance of the Person of Christ and remembrance of the Passion of Christ.

---

[22] The word group includes *anamimnēskō, anamnēsis, epanamimnēskō, mnaomai, mimēskō, mnēma, mnēia, mnēmeion, mnēmē, mnēmoneuō, mnēmosunon, hupomimnēskō,* and *hupomnēsis.*

First, remembering the Person of Christ: The grammatical case of "Me" indicates that it is the direct object of the verbal noun *remembrance*. We might translate the phrase "Do this for the purpose of remembering Me." Thus we understand that the table is intended to be a memorial of Jesus.

Memorials

At the time Jesus spoke these words it was not uncommon for great leaders to spend a lifetime and a fortune on building their *mnēma* or *mnēmeion* (grave, tomb, lit. *place of remembrance*). The huge Egyptian pyramids were built as burial chambers for the great pharaohs. Travelers who have been privileged to view the amazing tombs carved into the walls of the red sandstone of the city of Petra in Jordan have seen this first hand. The rock walls of that great valley are arrayed with 50-100 ft. high structures that look like Roman buildings with ornate roof structures and columns, but are actually sepulchers carved into the walls of the canyon. The ancient Nabataean kings would commission a crew of stone masons to begin carving their burial chambers into the mountain side as soon as they took power. These magnificent red rock monuments remain for visitors to view 2500 years later as samples of the ancient art of stone masonry, but the memory of the departed kings has long since faded.

Important Greek personages of means often chose to endow a memorial meal:

> It was not uncommon for those who could afford it, to leave in their last will and testament a stipend and stipulation that there be a memorial feast in honor of the deceased. Diogenes Laertius records *(10.16-22)* that Epicurus left provision for an annual celebration "in memory of us." [23]

Even St. Paul's Cathedral in London is a *mnēma* of sorts. The magnificent structure contains numerous monuments erected to the memory of some of the greatest personages of the British empire. The remains of its architect, Sir Christopher Wren, lie interred beneath a granite slab near a Latin inscription: *Lector si monumentum requires circumspice*—"If you would see his monument, look about you."

---

[23] Ben Witherington III, "Making a Meal of it: The Lord's Supper in Its First-Century Social Setting" in *Lord's Supper: Believers Church Perspectives*, ed. Dale R. Stoffer, Scottdale, PA: Herald Press, 1997, p. 100

But Jesus knew that death would only be able to keep Him interred in a rock tomb for three short days, and then its grip on His glorious body would be broken. Ever after, there would be no *mnēma*, no tomb for a *place* of remembrance, so He ingeniously crafted an *anamnēsis*, an *action* of remembrance, that would be able to withstand the ravages of time and be forever fresh to all who would gather at His table anywhere around this earth.

1. Remembering His Person—Facial Recognition Memory

Memory experts uniformly agree that facial memory is one of the most precise and remarkable features of our capacity to remember. Some assert that we never forget a face. What is even more remarkable is that we can spot family traits in people's faces (Oh, she looks just like her dad...)—and we do it instantly. Scientists uniformly assert that no computer could ever be built which can recognize faces like this. Those of us who are growing older find that we can instantly recognize a face that we haven't seen for decades when it is suddenly brought to our attention by a photograph. When our facial recognition memory connects with a person from our past, we find our mind immediately beginning to search for the cognitive details associated with the person represented by that face. This is the reason newspapers and magazines print photos of people's faces. This is the reason police use lineups for finding criminals. We recognize them. Faces stir our desire to find out more about a person. Some of us (including me) actually summon memories of people by seeing their face in our mind's eye.

But how can we truly remember Jesus' face if we never actually saw Him in the flesh? We would certainly never forget His face if we had seen it, as the couple from Emmaus saw it. We would never forget the face of the risen Savior if we had touched His wounded hands and felt the nail holes in His feet, as Thomas likely did. But, alas! We have not had the privilege of such a face to face encounter. We are part of the great multitude of whom He spoke when He addressed Thomas that night:

> ...Because you have seen me, you have believed; blessed are those who have not seen and yet have believed (John 20:29).

Thus, one of the challenges confronting us as we gather at His table is to have our senses stimulated to open our mind's eye of faith to truly see Jesus—and have our facial recognition memory come alive. Our beloved Lord and Savior bursts onto the screen of our visual recognition register, and we

37

meet Him at the table. What the Apostle Paul describes in 2 Cor. 4:6 becomes experiential reality:

> For God, who said, "Let light shine out of darkness," made his light shine in our hearts to give us the light of the knowledge of God's glory in the face of Christ.

So this first aspect of remembering Jesus is a very personal, intimate, face-to-face encounter with Him. It's the stuff of a vital love relationship. It's allied to what Paul hints at when he says, "I want to *know* Christ" (Phil. 3:10, italics mine).

2. Remembering His Passion—Cognitive and Episodic Memory

The second aspect of what it means to remember Jesus is about understanding what He did, remembering His passion. Whereas the former calls up our facial recognition memory, this latter aspect energizes our cognitive and episodic memories (related to the sequence of events). This dimension of remembering Jesus means *to remember what He did to redeem us.* It grows out of three important details of the narrative: 1) Jesus' declaration that the table proclaims His death, 2) the setting of the Passover, and 3) the meaning of the bread and cup.

1 Cor. 11:26 states plainly that those who eat and drink at the table proclaim (*katangellō*, often translated preach)—the Lord's death. By this Jesus doesn't mean that we simply publish the fact that He expired, but rather that we joyfully announce the good news that salvation has come through His redemptive death. This is the very setting of the Last Supper. The disciples were gathered with Jesus in an upper room to "eat the Passover" (Matt. 26:17). They were observing the time-honored traditional Seder which went back to the days of Moses fourteen hundred years earlier. The Passover was the story of God's miraculous redemption of His people through the blood of an innocent lamb, memorialized by a meal of bread and wine. Jesus blessed the third in the round of four cups of wine which had been labeled by the ancient rabbis as "the cup of redemption." Then He passed it and identified it with His own blood.[24] In addition, it was evidently the remnants of the un-

---

[24] Both Paul and Luke indicate that the cup Jesus transformed into the communion cup was "the cup after supper" (1 Cor. 11:25, Luke 22:20). This provides a strong linkage to the third of the four cups of the Seder which was called the Cup of Redemption in the rabbinic Haggadah.

leavened loaf which had been broken earlier in the Seder to which Jesus affixed the identity of His own body. That piece of bread pictured the messianic identification with the sinful human condition and His brokenness to remedy it.

Thus, the Last Supper was clearly all about Jesus' redemption. Remembering Him at His memorial table is also all about recalling the events of the cross and their meaning for us today.

Memory in the Life of Ancient Israel—the Contribution of Brevard Childs

Now let's probe the Jewish background surrounding the notion of remembrance. In a definitive study entitled *Memory and Tradition in Israel*, noted Semitic scholar Brevard Childs delves deeply into the ancient near eastern cultural understanding of memory. He shows quite convincingly that in the period of the Old Testament, remembering was never viewed as a mere passive storage of mental information; rather it always spurred action. He quotes J. Pederson:

> "When the soul remembers something, it does not mean that it has an objective memory image of some thing or event, but that this image is called forth in the soul and assists in determining its direction, its action…. The peculiarity about the Israelite is that he cannot at all imagine memory, unless at the same time an effect on the totality and its direction of will is taken for granted."[25]

Childs cites a number of examples from Homer's *Illiad and Odyssey* in support of this idea:

> Several idioms occur in which the verb [remember] is used to denote an action. To remember one's father and mother means to take care of them (Od. 18.767); to remember rest is to go to sleep (Od. 16.481); to remember the evening meal is synonymous with preparing the supper (Il. 24.601); to remember the dead means to bury them (Il. 22.390). Moreover, there are two expressions which occur with great frequency in Homer and illustrate the same point. When the Achaeans 'think of battle' (μνήσαντο δὲ χάρμης) they again experience the lust for battle (Il. 4.222;

---

[25] Quoted in Brevard S. Childs, *Memory and Tradition in Israel*, London: SCM Press Ltd., 1962, p. 17

8.252). This response is often viewed as part of the actual combat (Il. 15.380). Again, there is the expression 'remember the shield of valour' μνήσασθε δὲ θούριδος αλκης (Od. 4.527; Il. 8.174; 11.566). The phrase occurs regularly in speeches of encouragement. When men remember their past victories, they are spurred on to renew the fighting.[26]

This is also illustrated by the way God remembers His people in the Old Testament. He does not simply hold them in His *objective* memory, able to recall them at some future time. Rather, when God remembers, He *subjectively* feels their plight and honors His promise to comfort and redeem them. Jer. 31:20 well illustrates how God's memory of His people stirs His emotions:

"Is not Ephraim my dear son, the child in whom I delight? Though I often speak against him, I still remember him. Therefore my heart yearns for him; I have great compassion for him," declares the LORD.

Childs notes: "God's remembering always implies his movement toward the object of his memory."[27] He points out that the Old Testament is replete with examples of God remembering and taking action. For example, notice His compassion on barren Rachel:

Then God remembered Rachel; he listened to her and enabled her to conceive (Gen. 30:22).

Those who heard Jesus say "Do this in remembrance of Me" understood that they were being called to *act* upon the memory of Jesus. They were not being asked to simply conjure up mere sentimental objective memories of Jesus, fondly reminiscing about "the good old days." Rather, they were being called to remember with their wills, to go from the table with a calling upon their lives which had been summoned by the memory of their Savior. This action-oriented view of memory correlates with what we discussed above concerning the memories of the person of Christ.

The work of Childs also addresses another facet of memory in the life of ancient Israel. It correlates significantly with the second aspect of memories we considered above concerning the passion of Christ and the events surrounding our redemption. He examines the meaning of Israel's festivals which were designed to evoke remembrance, particularly the Sabbath. He notes that in Exodus the Sabbath command is based on remembering God as Creator

---

[26] Childs, p. 25
[27] Childs, p. 34

(Ex. 20:8-11), but in Deuteronomy it is premised upon remembering God as Redeemer (Deut. 5:13-15). The Deuteronomy text reads:

> Six days you shall labor and do all your work, but the seventh day is a Sabbath to the LORD your God. On it you shall not do any work…. Remember that you were slaves in Egypt and that the LORD your God brought you out of there with a mighty hand and an outstretched arm. Therefore the LORD your God has commanded you to observe the Sabbath day.

Childs points out that the weekly observance of the Sabbath was, in part, intended by God to arouse and incite memories of Israel's days of slavery in Egypt, in much the same way the annual Passover did. He says:

> Memory has a critical function of properly relating the present with the past. This critical role is confirmed by its frequent parallelism with the verb בִּין (byn, discern, consider, Deut. 32.7; Isa. 43.18, etc.).[28]

In other words, God wanted His people to observe a present-day activity which would *cause them to think about the meaning* of the distant deliverance at the Exodus. Even more, it would cause them to actually relive those events as though they had been there.

> When Israel observes the Sabbath in order to remember the events of her redemption, she is participating again in the Exodus event. Memory functions as an actualization (*Vergegenwärtigung*) of the decisive event in her tradition. The sign of the continuing relationship of Yahweh to his people is the rest of the Sabbath. Israel in every generation remembers and so shares in the same redemptive act.[29]

Childs later expands his definition of this long German word (*Vergegenwärtigung*, or actualization), and in so doing, makes observations which are exceptionally relevant to the way we gather at the table to remember Christ's redemptive acts of two thousand years ago:

> …the role of actualization [is] the recital in the cult of the great historical acts of the past which established Israel's existence. These acts share the quality of genuine historical events and are, therefore, non-repeatable, once-for-all in character. Actualization occurs when the worshipper expe-

---

[28] Childs, p. 54
[29] Childs, p. 54

riences an identification with the original events. This happens when he is transported back to the original historical events. He bridges the gap of historical time and participates in the original history.[30]

Thus, if we allow Childs' assessment of what it meant to remember an historical redemptive event, we conclude that Jesus was asking us to do more than simply recite the fact that He suffered and died when we gather at the table. He was asking us to be transported back to the foot of the cross and feel His suffering and see His eyes of love forgiving His tormentors. He was calling us to experience the awful separation He endured when the Father forsook His Son. He was asking us to feel the crushing weight of sin's depravity. He was inviting us to enter into the joyful cry of freedom of hopeless slaves being liberated. He was telling us to go back and experience what happened at the cross and feel its potency in the present. Says Merle Strege: "*Anamnēsis …* is the process of identification with this past event such that it becomes our event and determinative of our character."[31]

Let's summarize Childs' thesis in *Memory and Tradition in Israel:* To remember a person in ancient Israel was to take appropriate action. To remember an ancient redemptive act was to enter into its details in such a way as to contemporize it and experience its meaning in the here and now.

Retrieval Cues—the Sensory Stimuli to Summon the Word of God

Memory experts employ the language of the theater to describe the way we recall information stored in our memories. They compare the way we summon a memory to the way actors receive cues from the lines of other actors and the events happening on stage. Thus we speak of *retrieval cues* that call up stored memories. Retrieval cues come from our own internal thoughts as well as external sensory stimuli. They find a match with what we called retrieval tabs in chapter three, and somehow engage our supernaturally-designed capacity to summon the stored information.[32] Let's observe three New Testament examples of memory being retrieved. Let's notice how Luke,

---

[30] Childs, p. 82

[31] Merle D. Strege, "Ecclesiology and the Lord's Supper: The Memorial Meal of a Peaceable Community" in *Lord's Supper: Believers Church Perspectives*, ed. Dale R. Stoffer, Scottdale, PA: Herald Press, 1997, p. 127

[32] In all the scientific literature I have surveyed, I find universal confession of ignorance about how this amazing process of memory recall actually happens. I must personally fall back upon the Biblical assertion that we are made in the image of God, and as such, our minds echo His great ability to remember.

the author in each case, points out the kinds of retrieval cues which summoned memories of Jesus and spurred action.

•Peter and the crowing rooster—Jesus had informed Peter just hours earlier that he would be ashamed of Him and deny Him three times before a rooster crowed. Luke records the third denial and then Peter's remembrance:

> Peter replied, "Man, I don't know what you're talking about!" Just as he was speaking, the rooster crowed. The Lord turned and looked straight at Peter. Then Peter remembered the word the Lord had spoken to him: "Before the rooster crows today, you will disown me three times." And he went outside and wept bitterly (Luke 22:60-62).

The retrieval cues were sensory: he *heard* the rooster and *saw* the look of loving sadness in Jesus' eyes. His action (bitter weeping) proved that the remembrance found its way deep into Peter's soul. The memory carried a palpable emotional component.

•The women at the tomb—They *saw* and *touched* the empty tomb; they *heard* the voice of the angel tell them:

> "He is not here; he has risen! Remember how he told you, while he was still with you in Galilee: 'The Son of Man must be delivered over to the hands of sinners, be crucified and on the third day be raised again.'" [And, with all these poignant sensory retrieval cues,] [t]hen they remembered his words (Luke 24:6-8).

This remembrance radically and permanently changed their lives and those of countless others who were enabled to connect the sensory events of the resurrection with the previous words of Jesus and the scriptures. John records a similar statement:

> After he was raised from the dead, his disciples recalled what he had said. Then they believed the Scripture and the words that Jesus had spoken. (John 2:22)

•Peter and the vision of unclean animals—Peter *saw* the vision of the unclean animals; he *heard* God tell him it was OK to eat them; he *witnessed* the amazing timing of the men sent by Cornelius showing up at the conclusion of the vision; he *heard* Cornelius respond to the gospel; he *saw* and *heard* the Holy Spirit bring tongues to the new believers; and then he reports:

Then I remembered what the Lord had said: "John baptized with water, but you will be baptized with the Holy Spirit" (Acts 11:16).

This remembrance was responsible for the gospel finally leaving the confines of Jerusalem and beginning to penetrate the world of Gentiles. These examples show us how sensory input provided retrieval cues which summoned previously stored information about Jesus, and particularly His spoken Word. The memories recalled in this manner stirred deep emotion and spurred determined action.

A personal story will help illustrate how this works in our lives today. Some years ago I needed to do some plumbing repair in the upstairs attic of our home. The work required me to turn off the water on the ground level, climb a flight of stairs, climb a ladder into the crawl space of the attic, and then crawl on my belly through the dusty insulation to the place where the pipes were located. I am not a skilled plumber, and so the project took the usual three trips to the supply store while the water was turned off to the house. I made many trips up and down, and each time I was rubbing more dust off of the ceiling joists. On the final triumphant trip when I turned on the water and returned to find that my repair was not leaking, I suddenly saw something that immediately jarred my mind and instantly opened a fountain of tears to flow from my eyes. My travels across the joists had uncovered a board with a single word on it scrawled with a carpenter's keel (like blue crayon). It was my dad's unmistakable handwriting, and it said, "Pattern."

Before my conscious mind could unravel what was happening, I was deeply emoting and feeling the pain of my father's loss. He had died about a year earlier, and he had helped me build that part of the house. He had cut the rafters by making copies of a pattern rafter. Evidently we made one too many rafters, and the pattern rafter didn't get used, so it went into bracing the ceiling joists.

There it was: my dad's life, yanked up from my memory by the sudden sight of the word "pattern." I lay there in the attic for about five minutes just weeping and feeling the power of his remembered presence. As the emotions calmed, I began realizing that my dad had been the pattern for so many aspects of my life—and now God was telling me it was my turn to be the pattern to others whom God places in my path. My life has been altered by the sudden retrieval of that memory of my dad. I believe this is exactly what God intends to happen at the table when He stirs up memories of Jesus there.

God's Message Made Memorable

Not only are the senses involved in *summoning* stored memories; they are also significantly responsible for laying them down in the first place. The scriptures abound with examples of God making His message extremely memorable by enriching the communication with a number of—what I have called—multisensory retrieval tabs (see chapter three). When He wanted to ensure that His word would be hard to forget, He seized the senses, thus making the message intensely vibrant and memorable.

Take, for example, Moses' encounter with God at the burning bush (Ex. 3-4). Not only was God calling Moses to be the man who would extricate His people from bondage and lead them into the promised land, He was also revealing Himself as the covenant-keeping God known as "I am that I am." This was pretty heady stuff, and not something to forget via the Ebbinghaus curve! So God powerfully engaged most of Moses' senses. The episode began with his attention being drawn to the bush blazing in the middle of the desert and yet not burning up. He *saw* it and probably *smelled* the smoke and sulfurous fumes of the oily plant and likely *heard* the vicious crackling of the fire and *felt* its searing heat. Then he *heard* the voice of God telling him to take off his shoes. This meant that he had to *touch* his shoes and probably touched the ground at the same time as he fell to his knees in the awesome presence of the Holy One. At that point, God had his attention and delivered His self-revelation and call to Moses.

We will discover in our study of memory in succeeding chapters that *attention* is a key to the storage of long term memories, and attention gained through a *synesthetic experience* will cause the memory to be stored with many sensory retrieval tabs. Hence the memory will endure and be retrievable via a number of retrieval cues in the future.

I think it is fair to assume that Moses' memory of his encounter with God in the wilderness near Mt. Horeb was deeply encoded. It became the spiritual foundation for much of his future experience with God and His people. I suspect one of the main reasons it "stuck" so profoundly was the multisensory context in which the memory was first encoded.

Let's consider another example. When God was ready to begin the new and radically different era of the church on the day of Pentecost, He made His message very memorable by loading it with multisensory phenomena (Acts 2). Luke records that as the Spirit came upon the people they *saw* tongues of fire (and perhaps *heard* the crackling of the fire?), they *heard* the sudden roar of a stormy wind coming down out of the sky, and they *heard* people loudly praising God in languages they had never learned. Although the text doesn't specifically say so, I infer that they also *felt* the whole place rumbling under the influence of God's powerful presence. All of this seized their *attention* and allowed the message delivered by Peter that day to find its way deeply into the hearts—and memories—of the witnesses of these phenomena.

Consider, also, Paul's experience on the road to Damascus (Acts 9). On this occasion, God's message called Paul away from his Judaistic life of persecution and into the fellowship of serving Jesus. It was radical and powerful, and was rendered memorable by a very synesthetic experience. The fact that Acts twice records Paul recounting the details tells us that he never forgot it. It began with what he *saw*, first with a dazzling light, and then with scaly blindness. He *heard* God speaking out of the bright light. He *felt* his horse rear and throw him to the ground, which would certainly bring the *smell* of road dust into his nostrils. Then for the next three days, as he went without food or drink, he certainly *tasted* the unpleasantness of faster's mouth. All of these primed and honed his attention to hear the words of Jesus calling him to Himself.

If we reflect upon the story of redemption itself, we realize the incarnation was God's message packaged in a synesthetic bundle. To make the message of love and forgiveness clear and memorable, He sent His Son to come and dwell among us, bringing Him within the range of our senses. John specifically describes this as he begins his first epistle:

> That which was from the beginning, which we have heard, which we have seen with our eyes, which we have looked at and our hands have touched—this we proclaim concerning the Word of life. The life appeared; we have seen it and testify to it, and we proclaim to you the eternal life, which was with the Father and has appeared to us (1 Jn. 1:1-2).

It's not surprising then, to find the early apostles identified as those who had been with Jesus (Acts 4:13). This so impacted them they were unstoppable in their testimony about Him. They boldly declared: "As for us, we cannot help speaking about what we have seen and heard" (Acts 4:20).

We could look at many other instances of God's message made memorable through synesthesia (e.g. the masterful miracles of Jesus), but what we have seen is sufficient to establish the point. God, the masterful Creator and Designer of our capacity to remember, has, by His own example, shown us how to store enduring memories of His message.

So, What Does it Mean to Remember Jesus at the Table?

Let us now pull together the various strands of thought we have considered in this chapter to summarize what it means to remember Jesus at His table based on the exegetical meaning of *anamnēsis*:

Our observance of the Lord's table should:

- •Happen often and repeatedly enough to fend off the wolves of forgetfulness;
- •Include the active participation of the celebrants, not mere passive watching;
- •Awaken personal remembrances of Jesus Himself that stimulate a life of service (remembering the person of Christ);
- •Promote a connection to the events of redemption which carry us back—allowing us to experience them as though we were there—and then applying them to the circumstances of our daily lives now (remembering the passion of Christ);
- •Awaken our senses to summon previously stored memories of Jesus—even though we have never been privileged to actually see Him in the flesh;
- •Impact our senses to lay down new and more accurate memories of Jesus and the truth of the scriptures.

This is what we hope to accomplish via the simple meal of bread and wine taken in the communal gathering of the Body around the table.

Put another way, our participation in the bread and cup and all the surrounding sights, sounds, and ambiance should regularly prompt us to vividly see life-changing images of Jesus in our minds' eyes. They should all work together to enable us to emotionally and spiritually touch and connect with Him Who died for us. This remembrance will be evoked in our minds by the stimulation received through the antennae of our minds, the senses. These sensory inputs, along with the clear and accurate proclamation of the Word of God, will work together to accomplish two things: They will stimulate our minds to *create new, accurate* memories about who Jesus is and what He did, and they will *retrieve* and *correct* old memories already stored in our minds. Such vivid, compelling, multisensory images of the Savior experienced at the Lord's table can then in turn cause our minds to form and store a more perfect picture of Jesus. This vivid remembering will then prompt us to respond to Him in love, repentance, faith, obedience, etc.—the acts of true worship which should result from remembering Jesus. Beyond this, it will enhance the richness and accuracy of the memories to be retrieved the *next* time we gather in remembrance of Him.

Now we need to look a little more closely at the way our memories work in harmony with our senses.

*   *   *   *   *

Chapter 5
Sensational Memory

Amnesia

In the first frame of a classic *Peanuts* cartoon, Lucy, sitting at her desk in school, enthusiastically raises her hand to answer the teacher's question, blurting out, "I know the answer!" However, when the teacher actually calls on her in the second frame, with chagrin she is forced to admit, "But now I've forgotten it…" In the final frame, with characteristic Charles Shultz wryness, she muses, "Hard to explain how the human mind works, huh, Ma'am?"

Hard indeed, Lucy!

We are fearfully and wonderfully made in the image of our majestic Creator, and part of the remarkable echo of His own personhood which He bestowed upon us is a mind with the capacity to think and remember. Alas, we frequently share Lucy's frustration over our periodic lapses of memory, but what should amaze us far more is that most of the time we actually *are* able to remember things. Human consciousness and the attendant capacity to remember is what sets us far apart from all of the rest of God's creation. Our ability to remember is directly responsible for our awareness of self. Years ago, Samuel Johnson said, "It is indeed the faculty of remembrance which may be said to place [humans] in the class of moral agents."[33]

As a Bible student and teacher, I have learned that one of the ways to get at the meaning of complex abstractions and linguistic concepts is to look at their opposites, their antonyms. For instance, to understand *light*, it is exceptionally instructive to study *darkness*. So to get a glimpse of the depth and meaning of memory, it will be helpful to ponder what it would be like to have no capacity to remember. Let's look at the world of amnesia. This is, in fact, the way much of the psychological research has been conducted which has illuminated our still very limited understanding of memory.

With poignant insight, Nobel prize-winning author Gabriel Garcia Marquez explores the implications of human existence without memory. In his novel, *One Hundred Years of Solitude*, a contagious plague invades the small village of Macondo in Spain. Its first symptom is insomnia, but then as the disease progresses, those who are sick steadily lose aspects of their memories. First,

---

[33] Quoted in Philip Hilts, *Memory's Ghost*, NY: Simon and Schuster, 1995, p. 15

they lose their ability to call up childhood recollections; then they lose the names and functions of the objects around them. Soon they are unable to identify other people, and finally, says Marquez, each victim loses "even the awareness of his own being."[34]

As the story goes, a silversmith named Aureliano is confronted with the onset of his amnesia when he tries to find his familiar anvil. The resulting cascade of events vividly dramatizes the crucial role of memory in the functioning of our daily lives.

> One day he was looking for the small anvil that he used for laminating metals and he could not remember its name. His father told him: "Stake." Aureliano wrote the name on a piece of paper that he pasted to the base of the small anvil: *stake*. In that way he was sure of not forgetting it in the future. It did not occur to him that this was the first manifestation of a loss of memory, because the object had a difficult name to remember. But a few days later he discovered that he had trouble remembering almost every object in the laboratory. Then he marked them with their respective names so that all he had to do was read the inscription in order to identify them. When his father told him about his alarm at having forgotten even the most impressive happenings of his childhood, Aureliano explained his method to him, and Jose Arcadio Buendia put it into practice all through the house and later on imposed it on the whole village. With an inked brush he marked everything with its name: *table, chair, clock, door, wall, bed, pan.* He went to the corral and marked the animals and plants: *cow, goat, pig, hen, cassava, caladium, banana.* Little by little, studying the infinite possibilities of a loss of memory, he realized that the day might come when things would be recognized by their inscriptions but that no one would remember their use. Then he was more explicit. The sign that he hung on the neck of the cow was an exemplary proof of the way in which the inhabitants of Macondo were prepared to fight against loss of memory: *This is the cow. She must be milked every morning so that she will produce milk, and the milk must be boiled in order to be mixed with coffee to make coffee and milk.* Thus they went on living in a reality that was slipping away, momentarily captured by words, but which would escape irremediably when they forgot the values of the written letters.[35]

---

[34] Gabriel Garcia Marquez, *One Hundred Years of Solitude*, NY: HarperCollins Publishers, 1991, p. 45
[35] Marquez, p. 48-49

It is particularly fascinating that as his memory fades, Jose, Aureliano's father, a devout man of faith, not only labeled the *objects* of his life, but he also posted signs to remind him of his *beliefs*:

> At the beginning of the road into the swamp they put up a sign that said MACONDO and another larger one on the main street that said GOD EXISTS.[36]

This heroic attempt to label all the objects, feelings, processes, faces, and beliefs of life culminated in an ingenious memory machine which Jose constructed:

> The artifact was based on the possibility of reviewing every morning, from beginning to end, the totality of knowledge acquired during one's life. He conceived of it as a spinning dictionary that a person placed on the axis could operate by means of a lever, so that in very few hours there would pass before his eyes the notions most necessary for life.[37]

At this point in the story, the village was mercifully delivered from the plague by the magic potion of a gypsy whom Aureliano's father thought was a stranger, but whom he immediately recognized as an old familiar friend as soon as his memory returned.

> He gave José Arcadio Buendia a drink of a gentle color and the light went on in his memory. His eyes became moist from weeping even before he noticed himself in an absurd living room where objects were labeled, and before he was ashamed of the solemn nonsense written on the walls, and even before he recognized the newcomer with a dazzling glow of joy.[38]

Commenting on this story, noted Harvard memory expert, Daniel Schacter, observes:

> The novel dramatizes a world without memory: a world in which even close friends and family members seem like strangers; a world in which symbolic forms of communication are useless, and most of the tasks on which society depends cannot be performed; and, perhaps most tellingly, a world in which our sense of personal identity and self-awareness is stripped away. The narrator in Saul Bellow's *The Bellarosa Connection*, who

---

[36] Marquez, p. 49

[37] Marquez, p. 49

[38] Marquez, p. 50

runs a memory-improvement institute, sums it up for his clients: "Memory is life."[39]

Without memory there is no conceptual understanding, no ability to reason abstractly, and no observance of the Lord's table. Memory is the very core of human intelligence because all thinking and reasoning depends upon *comparing* and *contrasting* new sensory information with already stored knowledge and memories, by reasoning from *percept* to *concept* (as I said previously). In the words of Marcel Proust, memory is really a "telescope aimed at time" or, as Schacter has called it, "mental time travel." [40] No matter how they have lost their memory, whether by psychological distress or disease such as Alzheimer's or brain injury, one of the common denominators in all amnesiacs is their disorientation in time.[41] Events are bafflingly fragmented without meaningful sequence. Amnesiacs live in "the now" but lack the relative bearings to establish when "the now" is. Sensory information is fleeting, and the amnesiac lives with a confusing barrage of present moment experiences. Memory gives us a "time grid" from which to make sense of life—and more importantly, to make sense of the nature of Jesus' redemption. Thus I believe the Lord's table being aimed at our memories is not accidental. It is designed to cause us to peer through Proust's "telescope in time," first looking backward to the cross, then relating the cross to our present experience, and finally looking forward to the return of Christ ("you proclaim the Lord's death until He comes"). Observing the Lord's table requires our capacity to remember.

Amazing Memory Nestled in the Neurons of our Brains

Somehow—and herein lies one of the enormous mysteries of human existence—our mind and its seemingly inexhaustible capacity for memory has been nestled within the confines of the cells comprising our brains. As far as we understand it, the brain is the most complex object in the universe. Its roughly hundred billion cells, called neurons (from the Greek word meaning *string* or *sinew*), are constructed quite differently than the rest of the cells in our bodies. They are much longer than other cells and look like trees with massive umbrellas of branches on one end (called axons) and complex root balls on the other end (called dendrites). Axons are the senders of electrochemical messages and dendrites are the receivers. Each of these root and

---

[39] Daniel L. Schacter, *Searching for Memory*, NY: Basic Books, 1996, p. 2

[40] See Schacter, *Searching*, chapter one

[41] See many examples in Schacter, *Searching*, and Hilts who studies the well known case of George M. who had his hippocampus surgically removed to forestall the effects of epilepsy and became hopelessly amnesic.

branch structures can potentially connect to between 15,000 and 100,000 other dendrites and axons of other neurons making possible *hundreds of trillions* of signaling junctions, called synapses (from the Greek word meaning *clasp*). In one of the deepest hidden secrets known only to God, our magnificent Creator has somehow turned our mind loose to dwell among the interstices of this dizzying labyrinth. He has organized our memory—like a magnificent flock of birds—to somehow find nesting places for the events and ideas of our past among the incomprehensibly complex arrangement of neurons and their electro-chemical linkages.

Monroe Dodd depicts the amazing phenomenon of memory which somehow happens within the synapses of our brains this way:

> [I]n the tiniest place invisible to human eyes memory stores away words and sentences and books and laws and paintings and statuary and individuals and families and libraries and art galleries and cities and states and nations and races and countries and continents and worlds and stars and moons and suns. How marvelous is memory!

> Augustine said, "Great is this power of memory, exceeding great, Oh, my God. An inner chamber large and boundless. Who has plumbed the depths thereof ?"

> Memory is called the Mother of Muses because all the arts and sciences depend upon memory. It is, therefore, this citadel of the soul, this inner *sanctum sanctorum* of the mind to which Jesus lays claim and in which He asks the privilege of having a place.[42]

Indeed, Augustine was noted for his thoughtful reflections on the subject of memory:

> [I am in wonder and awe as I roam about in] the fields and spacious palaces of my memory, where are the treasures of innumerable images, brought into it from things of all sorts perceived by the senses. Hidden away in that place is whatever we think about.... When I enter there, I ask whatever I want brought forth, and something instantly comes; other things may be longer in coming, which are fetched, as it were, out of some inner receptacle; still others rush out in troops, and while one thing is desired and required, they start forth, each asking me, "Is it perchance I?" These I drive away with the hand of my heart, from the face of my

---

[42] Monroe E. Dodd, *Christ's Memorial*, Nashville: The Sunday School Board of the Southern Baptist Convention, 1934, p. 85

remembrance; until what I wish for be unveiled, and appears in sight, out of its secret place ….

There all things are preserved distinctly, each having entered by its own avenue: as light, and all colors and forms of bodies by the eyes; by the ears all sorts of sounds; all smells by the avenue of the nostrils; all tastes by the mouth; and by the sensation of the whole body, what is hard or soft; hot or cold; smooth or rugged; heavy or light; either outwardly or inwardly to the body. All these the great harbor of the memory receives in her numberless secret, and inexpressible windings. Each is brought out at need; each enters by his own gate, and is there laid up.[43]

The Naturalistic Explanation

In the midst of extolling the virtues of memory, Dodd affirms (and I concur): "No materialistic theory of the mind can explain the mystery of memory."[44] Yet this is precisely what modern secular science does. Most present day psychologists and neuroscientists join in the shrill atheistic chorus vehemently denying any non-material aspect of the mind. Their strident voices disparage any who would still cling to what they label "ancient outmoded superstitions." Mind, consciousness, thought, and memory, they say, have been scientifically proven to be nothing more than the perceived effects of synaptic firings of millions of neurons.

For example, a recent publication of Joseph LeDoux, a renowned neuroscientist at New York University, is entitled *Synaptic Self*. In it, he sets out to prove that the human self is "created and maintained by arrangements of synaptic connections,"[45] a purely physical phenomenon. This perspective, of course, grows out of the naturalistic evolutionary framework which permeates modern science. George Johnson believes that our minds are the result of the fittest surviving:

The brain is not likely to be a well-designed biocomputer whose flowcharts can be neatly laid out, but what Churchland [a noted philosopher/neuroresearcher] calls "a Rube Goldberg machine:" an accretion of evolutionary tricks for translating sensory data into mental structures—memories—that help ensure survival.[46]

---

[43] Quoted in Hilts, p. 59-60

[44] Dodd, p. 85

[45] Joseph LeDoux, *Synaptic Self*, NY: Vicking Press, 2002, p. 12

[46] George Johnson, *In the Palaces of Memory*, NY: Alfred A. Knopf, 1991, p. 223-224

This evolutionary philosophy actually leaks into the very terminology used by neuroscientists. One portion of the brain which is significantly connected to conceptual and semantic memory (the very kinds of thinking that reflect the image of God in humans) is named the *neocortex* (lit. *new rind* or *outer part*). It was given this name because other "lower" forms of life either don't have this structure, or, if they do, it is very much smaller and less functional. Hence the name *neocortex*, because, in the scheme of evolution, man's ability to think, talk, and reason developed very late.

William James, an early pioneer in evolutionary psychology (circa 1900), expressed this denial of an immaterial mind. Hilts (*Memory's Ghost*) quotes James as saying:

> In his essay "Does Consciousness Exist?" [William James] wrote that "There is ... no aboriginal stuff or quality of being, contrasted with that of which material objects are made, out of which our thoughts of them are made." Mind, including thought, and will, arises out of the physical order within the brain, and not from an infused soul. Mind stands not outside it, but within it. As flight is ascribed to the bird, thought is said to be a gesture of the brain.[47]

In summary, the secular scientific community looks at the wonderful ability of our minds to remember, and declares it to be nothing more than one of the many accidents allowing humans to survive and evolve to our present level of existence. Mind and memory, says modern science, are no more immaterial than the software program which enables the hardware of your computer to do the things it does. The popular modern scientific viewpoint ascribes all mental activity to the material brain. Secularists posit no abstract soul or mind, only neurons and axons and dendrites and synapses being modulated by neural transmitters. It's all electrical and chemical activity. But the Bible teaches something quite different....

Biblical View of the Mind and Memory[48]

The Bible denies the material-only model. It teaches plainly that our mind with its attendant capacity for memory is a remarkable echo of the very nature of God Himself, the Mind Who built the universe and conceived and carried out the plan of redemption. The Bible teaches that our mind has been

---

[47] Philip J. Hilts, *Memory's Ghost*, NY: Simon & Schuster, 1995, p. 74

[48] This discussion is a brief, over-simplified "thumbnail sketch" of the subject which occupies countless volumes in theological treatises. The reader is referred elsewhere for a detailed study.

sovereignly and intentionally placed within us as a central aspect of the immaterial part of our human nature.[49] It declares our "soul" or "mind" to be distinct from—and yet integrally intertwined with—our physical brain. Whereas the material-only model affirms that human consciousness ceases along with the death of the body, Christians believe that our mind/soul continues on forever.

The Bible repeatedly asserts that humans are created in the image and likeness of God (e.g. Gen. 1:26, 9:6, James 3:9). This significantly includes our mind and its marvelous capacity to remember. God knows, thinks, reasons, emotes, discerns, makes moral judgments, decides, and—important to our focus in this study—remembers. Amazingly, He imparted this same capacity to us, albeit in very limited and finite proportions in contrast to His infinitude. The newly created minds of our first parents, Adam and Eve, were perfect though finite, devoid of any moral understanding of evil. When they chose to disobey God's clearly defined boundaries, sin entered the world. Their very natures were altered by the presence of sin and death, and this had particular impact upon their minds (and ours!). Ever since the fall into sin, human minds and hearts have been darkened by sin (Rom. 1:21, Eph. 4:17-18); they are depraved (Rom. 1:28); they have been blinded (2 Cor. 4:4). It is generally understood that this means we have faulty moral discernment, that we are unable to reason, think, remember, and make judgments with perfect reliability as evaluated against the standard of God's absolute righteousness and truth. This affects the accuracy and dependability of our memories. In our unregenerated condition, we have minds which reflect God's image, but it is a seriously darkened reflection.

However, the good news of the gospel of Jesus Christ is that we can be changed! When we are born again through faith in His atoning death, part of the newness God works in us (2 Cor. 5:17) directly impacts our minds. Paul joyfully declares that believers "have the mind of Christ" (1 Cor. 2:16) and are being "made new in the attitude of [their] minds" by the grace of God (Eph. 4:23). Eadie comments that this renewal of our mind means it is changed "in that which gives mind both its bent and its materials of

---

[49] Theologians debate *trichotomy* vs. *dichotomy*, whether humans have three parts (body, soul, and spirit) or two (material—i.e. body, and immaterial—including soul, spirit, heart, mind, and a host of other terms describing aspects of our non-material being). The debate is significant; however, for the purpose of this present study, it is irrelevant. Trichotomists typically view "the mind" as roughly equivalent to the soul, dividing the soul into intellect, emotion, and will. Dichotomists often view "the mind" similarly while also including the notion of "spirit" as part of the mind.

thought."[50] As we saw previously, the mind receives its "materials of thought" from two sources: sensory input and stored memories. Therefore, the healing of our depraved minds through the marvelous working of God's grace is intended to accomplish remedial work on our memory and on how we process sensory input. Through the faithful and powerful guidance of the Holy Spirit, believers can be enabled to more correctly evaluate sensory input and memories against the reliable standard of God's truth. I believe God planned the Lord's table to play a key role in that marvelous process of mental renewal.

Engraphy, Engrams, and Ecphory

Now let's turn our attention to the way our memories work. For the past 150 years, clinical psychologists have been probing the murky depths of our memories from a user's standpoint, roughly analogous to studying how a car performs on a test track. Neuroscientists, on the other hand, have been exploring the way memory works from the standpoint of physical changes in the brain's neurons and their linkages via electro-chemical neurotransmitters, somewhat analogous to studying the way a car's engine operates at the level of the pistons and sparkplugs. Neuroscience has greatly advanced our awareness of the staggering complexity of the brain's activity, and it has widened our understanding of the way different kinds of mental processes occur in different regions of the brain.[51] But neuroscience remains woefully inadequate in explaining the quantum leap from biochemical synaptic changes to the phenomenal reality of human consciousness and thought. PET scans and MRIs[52] clearly reveal localized and regional brain activity as "remembering"

---

[50] Quoted by M. R. Vincent, *Word Studies in the New Testament*, n.d. @ Eph. 4:23

[51] Schacter, (*Search*) summarizes some of the recent findings: "The frontal lobes are a vast territory consisting of distinct subregions that play important roles in such processes as elaborative encoding, strategic retrieval, working memory, and recall of source information…. Specific regions within the parietal, occipital, and temporal lobes participate in the storage of different aspects or attributes of long-term memories…. These cortical areas cooperate closely with structures in the inner sectors of the brain, such as the hippocampus,… to allow us to remember explicitly our ongoing experiences. The hippocampus, part of the limbic system, and the thalamus, part of the diencephalon, both play important roles in explicit remembering. The amygdala, also part of the limbic system, is critical for emotional memories…. The cerebellum, part of the hindbrain, is prominently involved in procedural memory." [p. 54 and 138]

[52] PET (positron emission tomography) and MRI (magnetic resonance imaging) are two of the current computerized research tools being used to watch the brain while it remembers.

takes place, but they have no way to explain who or what is guiding the process to locate the stored information. (It is my opinion that the seemingly incomprehensible intertwining of immaterial mind and material brain is one of the grand secrets of the Creator, Deut. 29:29.) It is, however, the research of the psychologists which has unearthed especially useful information pertinent to our study of the Lord's table.

Since earliest times, mankind has tried to understand the mysterious workings of memory. For example, Plato compared memory to the wax impression of a signet ring given to us by the goddess of memory:

> I would have you imagine, there exists in the mind of man a block of wax, which is of different sizes in different men; harder, moister, and having more or less purity in one than another, and in some of an intermediate quality.... Let us say that this tablet is a gift of Memory (Mnemosyne), the mother of the Muses [the Muses are the properties of the imagination, and Memory begets them all]; and that when we wish to remember anything which we have seen, or heard, or thought in our own minds, we hold the wax to the perceptions and thoughts, and in that material receive the impression of them as real, the seal of a ring; and that we remember and know what is imprinted as long as the image endures; but when the image is effaced, or cannot be taken, then we forget and do not know.[53]

Obviously, nowadays we recognize that memory is not a block of sealing wax. So what is it? Is it like a video file that contains the full and complete records of the events of our lives? Not likely, say the investigators. Extensive research has revealed it as a much more complex series of processes which synaptically store and retrieve bits and pieces of information in various ways and in various places within the brain.

Memory has three aspects or phases: the acquisition phase (known as engraphy—from Greek, *writing in*, also referred to as *encoding*), the storage phase (known as the engram—from Greek, *what is written in*), and the retrieval phase (known as ecphory—from Greek, *carrying out*). All three aspects are vital to the depth and accuracy of memories. The following diagram depicts a very simplified flow chart of how this process is currently understood by memory researchers.

---

[53] Quoted in Hilts, p. 49

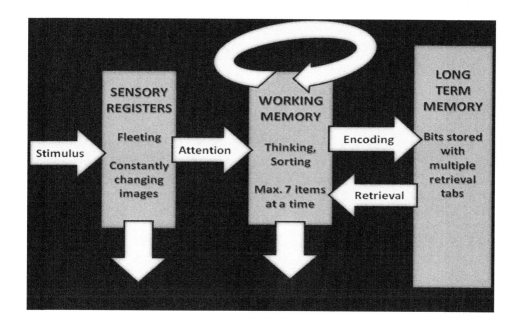

Sensory Memory

The wonderful phenomenon of memory begins with sensory input. We start out with basically blank memories when we are conceived, and all we learn and know and remember over time is acquired through what we see, hear, smell, touch, and taste.[54] The neurons of the brain have direct linkages to the neurons which register sensory stimuli in the skin, eyes, ears, nose, and mouth. They are linked to the texture and temperature registers of the skin via the spinal cord. The processes going on constantly within our organs of sense rendering environmental sights, sounds, smells, tastes, and tactile surfaces into meaningful synaptical messages are nothing short of mind-boggling miracles. But somehow, incredibly, we are enabled to see and hear and smell and taste and feel. Each sensory system has its own specially allocated region in the brain which marvelously records the firings of neurons. Here, in these so-called sensory registers of our brain, we see, hear, smell,

---

[54] There is some evidence that the new brain is not completely blank. For example, well known linguistic expert Noam Chomsky asserts that children are born with a biologically "hard-wired" predisposition for what he calls Universal Grammar. This, he asserts, is a body of linguistic knowledge that is common to all human languages. He suggests that the echoic percepts arriving in the young brain related to the specific language being spoken around the child resonate with portions of the Universal Grammar already present in the mind of the child. If Chomsky is correct, it shouldn't surprise followers of Jesus. He is the Word, and we are all created in His image. One key aspect of His image is the ability to communicate in words and ideas.

feel, and taste. The images flashing in the sensory registers are constantly shifting, lasting at the most a tenth of a second.

Not all sensory memory traces are equal. For example, *olfactory* images, the information coming from the smells reaching our noses, have a stronger priority and arrive at the place of our "working memory" (likely the part of the brain called the hippocampus) faster than *iconic* images, the scenes that are constructed from what our eyes see. We have all had the arresting experience of being suddenly catapulted back to a different time and place by the unexpected encounter of a long-forgotten fragrance.

The vast majority of information constantly barraging our senses is almost immediately discarded. Primarily that to which we give our attention is what continues to occupy our working memory.

Working Memory

The rather bland clinical term "working memory" refers to the staggering phenomenon of thought and consciousness constantly going on inside of us. As you are reading these words right now, with near lightning speed, your working memory is processing the incoming images brought to you by your eyes and is constantly summoning stored memories which connect the letter symbols to words you already know. Thus you are enabled to understand the message I have written here. Now test yourself: Without looking up, what did I say in the previous paragraph? If you are like most folks, perhaps you remember the gist, but the specific words are already discarded from your working memory. Such is the nature of our minds. On the other hand, if there was something in that last paragraph that really made you stop and think and rehearse the thought for several seconds, it is much more likely you still remember it now. Or perhaps you remembered an experience of sudden olfactory recall when the smell in a grocery store reminded you of your grandmother's house. In either case, you rehearsed the notions you had been reading, and the memory trace is much stronger.

Experts tell us our working memory can only hold about seven items at a time. New incoming information keeps shoving older stuff out. Working memory is a little like standing at a conveyor belt watching a parade of good food going by, and unless you reach out and grab an item, it just goes on by. According to those who study memory, the memory traces on that mental conveyor belt only last 15-20 seconds. After that they are discarded if we don't grab them. "Reaching" for the items brought into our working memory is another way of saying that we are paying attention.

Our parents and teachers always told us to pay attention, and they were on to something! Researchers have repeatedly shown that one of the most important factors in determining whether we will retain a memory is how much we pay attention, how much we focus our concentration. Says Schacter, "Our memory systems are built so that we are likely to remember what is most important to us."[55] Some of us (like my wife, Cathy) are blessed by the Creator with the capacity to keep several things going in working memory at once. I marvel at her "four-track mind." Others of us seem to be more limited—with what could be described as a "one-track mind." But whether you have one or four tracks, what you remember is greatly impacted by what occupies your attention.

Only recently have neurological investigators discovered the physiological basis behind the short life of sensory and working memories. They have found that the messages ferried across the synapses of the brain cells involved in short term memory (sensory and working memory) are purely electro-chemical and leave no physical modifications to the neurons themselves. In contrast, memories which persist and become more or less permanent involve actual material changes to the axons and dendrites of the neurons storing the engram. In the language of science: "[O]n the cellular level the switch from short-term to long-term facilitation is a switch from a process-based memory to a structural-based memory."[56] Neurons lengthen and permanently form new synapses with other neurons in response to the production of specific proteins as instructed by genes which guide the keeping of memories.

In other words, when we pay attention and rehearse a thought, the very neurons encoding the memory are physically changed. Neuroscientists call this long term potentiation. In fact, the more we rehearse and practice and think about something, the deeper and more durable becomes the engram. This is how Dr. Frank Minirth describes the process:

> Once an impulse crosses a synapse, the next impulse will cross much more readily. A path has been burned, so to speak, although the word *burned* is certainly inexact. The more the impulses cross a synapse, the easier such crossings become. This is what makes habits and thoughts in-

---

[55] Schacter, *Search*, p. 46
[56] Schacter, *Search, p. 83*

grained. The memory has been replayed so many times, it's burned in deeply.[57]

William James said:

> Of two men with the same outward experiences and the same amount of mere native tenacity, the one who thinks over his experiences most and weaves them into systematic relations with each other enhances recall.[58]

Neuroscience has learned that long term memories are stored in regions in the brain specifically devoted to the senses which originally acquired and processed the information. Thus a memory which has been stimulated by a multitude of sensory and thinking inputs will be stored in a multitude of places in the cerebral cortex.[59]

Working Memory and the Lord's Table

Thus we see that storage of memories requires more than casual attention; it depends on focused interest and rehearsal. It should be immediately apparent how pertinent and crucial this fact is to our observance of the Lord's table. If we are to gather with the expressed intention of remembering Jesus and not allow the sensory images and truth presented to be immediately discarded from our short term memories, then we must decide to pay careful attention and rehearse these things assiduously. How often have we met, taken the elements, prayed, sung a song, gone home… and because we didn't grab the food off the conveyor belt, it passed right on out of our working memory and never found its way into our long term memory? This fact alone may account for much of the "ho hum" attitude that pervades so many of our congregations when we gather at the table. We just haven't captured their attention, and so they haven't acquired the ability to encode the long term memories of Jesus. It is my desire in the remainder of this book to provide you with specific ways to get and keep their attention so that they will encode lasting and accurate memories of Jesus.

---

[57] Frank Minirth, *The Power of Memories*, Nashville: Thomas Nelson, 1995, p. 20

[58] Quoted in Alan Baddeley, *Your Memory: A User's Guide*, NY: McMillan, 1982, p. 110

[59] Kandel, *In Search of Memory*, p. 130

Long Term Memory and the Lord's Table

When we say these two little words, "I remember," we are living out one of the greatest miracles of human existence. Our mind has just completed a successful search of the hundreds of billions of information bits[60] tucked away within the windings of our brain cells for almost as long as we've been alive, and has retrieved that one item for our consideration. How we are enabled to do this is a secret known only to our Maker. But, nonetheless, we do it! If you haven't stopped and thanked God for your ability to remember recently, why don't you put the book down right now and do it.

How does our mind organize memories so they can be retrieved at a later date? Well, only our Creator knows for sure, but our best guess is that the memory bits are filed away in the reaches of the rear portion of our brains much like we file library books or computer files. It is believed that a good deal of this organizing takes place while we are asleep. Elizabeth Loftus, a noted secular memory expert, surprisingly describes the arrangement as the work of "a superb librarian" living inside our brains:

> Long-term memory is more or less thought of as a permanent storehouse of facts. It contains all the events of a lifetime. It is practically limitless, and there seems to be no risk of overloading long-term memory, which is remarkable given the relatively small space in our brains. But storage is not the problem. In order for this vast library of knowledge to be useful to us, there must be some plan or scheme to the way the information is arranged. Otherwise, we would not be able to find anything. Somewhere in each person's brain lives a superb librarian.

> How is long-term memory arranged? The analogy to a library and its card catalog, or to a book and its index, seems to be a useful one. The card catalog or book index is used as a way of finding any material that we need. Similarly, we use "indexes" to call up information that is cataloged in long-term memory. We might get to our memory of Aunt Beth's swimming pool by thinking of swimming pools in general or hearing the words our sister remarked, "Remember last summer at Aunt Beth's." The more ways we have to index a piece of information or the more associations we have with it, the easier it is to remember. It is important to keep in mind that we don't file away film clips or tape recordings of our experience. Rather, we store bits and pieces of our experience. A particu-

---

[60] Some estimates suggest our memories can assimilate one trillion bits in a lifetime!

larly happy birthday party may have lasted three hours, but if a friend took that long to tell you about it, you might find him quite dull indeed. The brain condenses experiences for us. It seems to edit the boring parts in order to highlight the interesting parts and cross-reference them for storage.[61]

Recalling something we "try" to remember, as Dr. Loftus has described, is called *associative* retrieval. It gets that name because we search our memory banks using retrieval cues that are *associated* with the retrieval tabs (what she calls indexing and cross-referencing) with which we stored the memory. Note that she pointed out a very significant characteristic of long term memory: "The more ways we have to index a piece of information or the more associations we have with it, the easier it is to remember." Others call this "elaborative encoding."[62] This has vitally important implications for our observance of the table. It means if we can assist our people in attaching many different associations to their memories of Jesus and His work of redemption, then we will aid them in better remembering Him.

Let me illustrate. If you have taken your people to the table and helped them to see Jesus through the story of the serpent Moses lifted up in the wilderness, then the next time they see a snake, it can facilitate a memory of Jesus Who conquered Satan at the cross. Or if you have led them through a Passover dinner and helped them to see Jesus as the Lamb of God, then the next time they read about or see a sheep, they should be able to summon memories of Jesus. Hence, one of our goals in leading our people to the table should be to help them attach as many retrieval tabs to the person and work of Jesus as possible.

Strategic Memory and the Lord's Table

Memory experts also refer to a second type of retrieval which is extremely pertinent to our observance of the table as well. It's called *strategic* retrieval or *trigger* recall. It's when a flash on our sensory register is an exact match with a stored memory, and suddenly—without conscious attempts to recall—we are overpowered with a startlingly clear memory. Olfactory memories (smells) are particularly subject to strategic recall because they have a shortened neurological pathway to the place of the working memory. Helen Keller, whose

---

[61] Loftus, p. 27
[62] Schacter, *Search*, p. 43-45

blindness and deafness provided no percepts from either her eyes or ears, paints a vivid verbal portrait of her olfactory memories:

> Smell is a potent wizard that transports us across thousands of miles and all the years we have lived. The odors of fruits waft me to my southern home, to my childhood frolics in the peach orchard. Other odors, instantaneous and fleeting, cause my heart to dilate joyously or contract with remembered grief. Even as I think of smells, my nose is full of scents that start awake sweet memories gone and ripening fields far away.[63]

Not long ago I opened an old book in my library, and I was suddenly transported back to an old hardware store in my hometown I hadn't seen for forty years. There was something in the smell of that old book which was an exact match with the smell in that old hardware store stored in my memory banks.

We experience strategic recall from visual (called *iconic*) memories as well. This is particularly true of faces. How often have you seen a person for the first time and found yourself saying, "She looks a lot like so-and-so?" Perhaps you haven't seen so-and-so for many years, but the iconic memory engram is there, and the new face has triggered an instant recall. The story I related in the previous chapter about my dad and the pattern rafter is another example of a visually triggered memory.

These "jack-in-the-box" memories which come jumping out of their secret hiding places can be triggered by percepts from any and all of our senses. Sights, sounds, tastes, smells, and even textures, can unexpectedly unleash a memory buried for decades. Now let me ask you to stop and ponder how significant it would be if you could marshal this capacity for strategic recall as people gather around the Lord's table.

Sometime back, I watched an old movie called *Seasons of the Heart* about pioneer life in eastern Oregon around 1870. It is the story of a young boy named Daniel whose parents died in a plague that swept the prairie, and who is sent to live with a new family. He misses his mother terribly. The only tangible connection he has to his old family is contained in a small box he keeps near his bed. In a very touching scene, he is shown opening the box and taking out a small lock of his deceased mother's hair. Then he gently rubs the hair against his cheek. From the look on his face as the camera pans closer, it is

---

[63] Quoted in "Your Nose is a Camera" in Joan Steen Wilentz, *The Senses of Man*, NY: Crowell, 1968, p. 129

clear that the sight of that hair and its familiar smell and unique texture have summoned a moment of precious glimpses of his beloved mother.

Wouldn't it be awesome if you could, in the same way, help your people experience sights and smells and sounds and textures and tastes which trigger precious glimpses of Jesus at His table? Keep reading.

Six Factors Influencing Long Term Memory Storage and Retrieval

Now although we have no so-called "cogniscope," or viewer to actually watch our memories while they are being stored and retrieved secretly inside our brains, neuroscience and psychological research *have* learned a great deal about the things which influence the process. Much of what has been discovered is incredibly helpful in our quest to revitalize the Lord's table. What follows is a compilation of findings concerning things which influence and enhance memory storage and retrieval with specific application to enriching our experience of remembering Jesus.

1. Synesthesia and the Specific Role of the Various Senses

When we experience an event which is brought into our memories through more than one sensory register, the "librarian in our brains" is able to encode it with multiple retrieval tabs. Alan Baddeley says that this "synaesthesia, the capacity to make rich associations between images from the different senses, generally enhances perception and recall."[64] Remember in the previous chapter we saw examples of God using this approach when He had a message for His people He wanted to make "stick" in their memories.

Let me illustrate: When we simply hear a preacher *talking* about the price of our redemption, the potential for significant long term memory storage is greatly minimized. However, when the message is also visualized with pictures of the crucifixion, there is potential for deeper encoding. Again, Baddeley points out that such "[d]ual encoding increases one's chances of remembering something."[65]

---

[64] Baddeley, p. 37 [note British spelling of synesthesia]
[65] Baddeley, p. 89

Delightfully, the Lord's table affords manifold opportunities for synesthesia because it is ideally suited to invoke *all* the senses. I believe a memorable gathering at the table will thoroughly engage the eyes of the participants, thus creating *iconic* memories. This will include both images of redemptive objects (e.g. sheep, crosses, animal sacrifice, the breaking of the bread, etc.) and redemptive scriptural texts either displayed on a screen or written on paper. Both are important because memory specialists tell us that different retrieval tabs are attached to objects (primarily processed in the right hemisphere of the brain) from those affixed to abstract written language (which is principally handled in the left hemisphere).

Extensive involvement of the sense of hearing, both of the clearly spoken word ("faith comes from hearing," Rom. 10:17) and of other sounds of redemption such as the sound of nails being driven, also enhance synesthesia. Our *echoic* memory (sounds) is particularly fitted for storing away familiar meaningful music. I believe music should play a central role in synesthetically encoding powerful glimpses of Jesus. More on this under "Importance of Emotion" below.

Memories involving touch, (called *haptic* memory) can be nurtured in many ways. For example, if the theme of the service is our unity in Christ (as presented by Paul in 1 Cor. 10:16-17), we might have our people holding each other's hands. Or we might have them take off their shoes and allow their bare feet to touch the floor imagining it to be the sand of the desert where Moses met God at the burning bush. One time I passed an ounce of pure gold around the room, inviting each person to feel its weight and smoothness. That Sunday I was talking about the inheritance which Jesus purchased in glory for us through His redemptive death. Of course, every time we take the elements we touch them. This was a source of great controversy in the days of the Reformation, as we mentioned above, and the reformers fought to restore this blessed privilege to the people. Catholic theologians argued that human hands were simply not worthy to touch the blessed "host." But the command of Jesus was to "*take* and eat." An old preacher responded quite eloquently to the Catholic prohibition:

> [O]ur mouths are as unworthy as our hands to receive Christ's body. But, seeing it is Christ's pleasure to come under the roof of our mouth, let Him also pass through the porch of our hands. The rather because it seemeth that we entertain Christ's body in more state, and with more observance towards it, when the more servants [i.e. body members and senses] attend it, the more members of our body using their service in re-

ceiving it…. The Romish custom loseth the significancy of the hand of faith. The taking Christ's body in our hands mindeth us spiritually by faith to apprehend and lay hold on His mercies and merits.[66]

For this reason, when I am presiding at the table, I have made it a practice to always lift the loaves before the people as I break them. I ask the participants to break off a piece of the bread for themselves as it is passed to them. In addition, at times I will request that they hold their personal morsel up before their eyes and inspect it, allowing the synesthesia of seeing and touching to have its full impact.

Of course, there is our wonderful sense of smell. As we have noted above, *olfactory* perceptions have an anatomical priority in summoning memories. I personally think we who lead the table need to ask God to give us creative ways to engage the powerful sense of smell. As we will see in chapter seven, when Jews at the time of Christ gathered around the Passover table, the smells were unmistakably pungent: bitter herbs, roasting lamb, freshly baked bread, aromatic wine. It is, admittedly, a significant challenge to marshal such aromas in our observance of the Lord's table, but we will find their mnemonic value to be well worth the effort. I have often encouraged the folks who were gathered around the table to hold the freshly broken bread to their nose for a moment and simply take in the sweet aroma of redemption.

Scientists affirm that we actually have more than the obvious five senses. One of them which is particularly relevant to our study is called the sense of proprioception. This is the sense that the brain depends upon to keep track of the body's orientation in space. It's the sense that doctors check when a person has suffered a blow to the head. They ask, "Where are you?" If the victim's sense of proprioception is working, the person knows where he/she is. Interestingly, memory researchers have found that we are better able to retrieve memories when we are located in the place where the memory was first formed. Says Baddeley, "Reinstating the environment in which an event was experienced will bring the memory of that event flooding back."[67] This is why it is so important for us to regularly affirm the gathering *around the table*. I make it a practice to set the room so that the table is always in the very center of focus. It is helpful to set the room differently from days when the table is not being observed. Shine a spotlight on the table. It should become immediately obvious to our people the moment they enter the room that they are

---

[66] T. Fuller, D.D. in Joseph Exell, *The Biblical Illustrator*, 1 Cor. Vol. II, Grand Rapids: Baker Book House (n.d.), p. 100
[67] Baddeley, p. 105

there to remember Jesus. Their sense of proprioception will "kick in," priming the pumps of their minds to bring forth memories of Jesus.

Finally, there is taste. The observance of the Lord's table culminates in eating the bread and drinking the cup. Similar to our sense of smell, taste is powerfully effective in eliciting memories. We all have experienced the sudden recall of events and places and people in our past as we take a bite of food, such as: "Oh, this reminds me of my mother's famous apple pie. I can see her now, in her tattered red apron with the big heart on the front, lovingly rolling out the dough." But taste is much more than just an excellent retrieval cue; *it is our sense of commitment*, the action of our physical life which parallels faith in our spiritual life. We can study the value of food by looking at it, smelling it, touching it, and even hearing it (e.g. the "snap, crackle, and pop" of Rice Krispies). But all of that is mere investigation. It is only when we actually take the morsel into our mouths and then swallow it that we have committed ourselves to its value. This is why ancient kings appointed a personal cupbearer (e.g. Nehemiah). It was his sobering responsibility to taste the king's food and drink before the king could potentially be poisoned.

Thus, to taste is to commit. Accordingly, it is extremely significant that the observance of the Lord's table should culminate in eating and drinking the physical elements which portray the spiritual food we have received by faith. We are in fact what we eat—both physically and spiritually. Before their fall into sin, Adam and Eve *ate* from the blessed Tree of Life, demonstrating that they were eternally righteous beings. Then in their fall they *ate* of the forbidden Tree of the Knowledge of Good and Evil, and were banished from ever eating of the Tree of Life again. Instead, they (and all their Old Covenant descendants) were required to offer regular animal sacrifices, of which the priests regularly *ate*, picturing their commitment to its spiritual value in dealing with their fallen condition. It should not surprise us then, that our celebration of the final redemptive solution of Adam's fall—the death of the Lamb of God—should involve *eating*. As Dr. Fuller pointed out above, at the Lord's table we dramatically do outwardly what we have already done inwardly: we reach out in faith and take what God has provided and then put it into our mouths. While the table itself is the drama of Christ's *work* of redemption, our taking of the elements is the drama of our own personal *experience* of that redemption.

In summary: seek to engage all the senses. This will allow the Holy Spirit to weave a beautiful tapestry in the minds of our audience with strands from what they have seen, heard, touched, smelled, oriented in space, and tasted.

On that tapestry—stored away in their long term memory—will be an awe-some picture of Jesus bristling with a multitude of varied retrieval tabs. We will be following in the footsteps of the Apostle Paul whose preaching so engaged the senses of his audience that he could later say, "Before your very eyes Jesus Christ was clearly portrayed as crucified" (Gal. 3:1).

2. Importance of Emotion

For a long time it has been observed that certain memories are powerfully stamped upon our long term memory when they are accompanied by strong emotional states.[68] For example, a tragic event such as the collapse of the Twin Towers on 9-11 will be replayed over and over again in our minds. The same holds true for very pleasant memories as well as those accompanied by intense states of anxiety, anger, or fear. More recently, however, science has discovered a physiological basis for this phenomenon. A small member within the brain called the amygdala controls the release of certain stress-related hormones such as epinephrine and adrenaline. These hormones actually improve the ability of the synapses to form lasting changes. They are released when our sensory registers encounter information which evokes emotional response. Thus the situations which cause us to feel sad or angry or happy also enable us to remember better.

Now we have to be extremely wise and cautious as we approach this point. The same emotion-induced hormones which help us encode vivid memories also can cause us to miss other peripheral details and create inaccurate and/or incomplete memories.[69] So for us who lead the table, creating emotion can become counterproductive if we are not scrupulously careful. We should never work to generate emotion for emotion's sake. Emotions, as God designed them, are simply flags that signal our awareness of the "goodness and badness" of both our outer environment and our inner well-being. Emotions are not always understood by our reasoning minds. Reasoning and logic occur primarily in the brain's temporal lobe. Emotions, in contrast, are almost entirely spawned in the regions called the amygdala and thalamus. Yet our emotions are created by God to enhance the texture of our lives—and the Lord's table—and hence we should embrace them as welcome friends whenever they emerge in our remembrances of Jesus.

---

[68] See for example Thomas H. Metos, *The Human Mind: How We Think and Learn*, NY: F. Watts, 1990, p. 91, and Minirth, p. 34
[69] Aamodt and Wang, *Welcome to Your Brain*, p. 101

The story of redemption as depicted at the table is replete with emotion. The condition of the human race in our lostness and death is enough to produce tears—it did in Jesus. The events of Jesus' passion and crucifixion are despicably awful and should evoke anger and grief. The sudden slash of a knife cutting the throat of an innocent lamb should cause our heads to turn away in horror. The shame of a naked slave being auctioned in a Roman slave market should enrage our sense of justice. The price of redemption was high, and the table is wringing wet with tears of pain and sorrow. Yet at the same time, the table is also the symbol of joy, freedom, love, righteousness, and hope. It embraces a most amazing juxtaposition of mourning and dancing, funeral dirges and victory chants, tears of sadness and tears of joy. If ever there was a supernaturally crafted place wherein the free expression of our capacity to emote was appropriate, it is certainly right here.

How do we properly encourage emotion at the table so that the memories of Jesus are enhanced? I think part of the answer comes in presenting the message truly and without compromise. We shouldn't be afraid to look at the actual practice of crucifixion. We shouldn't shy away from talking about the horrors of hell. We shouldn't hesitate to show Jesus agonizing in the Garden of Gethsemane, feeling the crushing weight of the sin of the world bearing down upon His shoulders. We shouldn't be afraid to encourage our people to celebrate their freedom with happy singing and clapping and even dancing. In other words, if we allow the message of Christ's love to be seen clearly, it will—*all by itself*—evoke emotion.

Another way to help our people emote at the table is through the prudent use of music. Music is unquestionably the language of the soul. Excellent communion music engages both our intellect and our emotions. The lyrics underscore the message being taught, and the tune finds it way deep into the right hemisphere and liberates emotions. I would love to have a "cogniscope" and see inside my brain while I am singing "When I Survey the Wondrous Cross." I can only imagine my amygdala being very active, because I usually find it very hard to sing without tearing up. That song pulls up deeply encoded memories of Jesus from within me.

I witnessed a powerful illustration of this as my dear mother was approaching her last days on this earth. She was in the final stages of her slow descent into the abyss of Alzheimer's, that vicious robber of memory. At that point in her disease she would sit in her wheelchair with her head bent forward limply as she stared off into the apparent meaninglessness around her. She seemed to have little or no contact with the world, and it seemed to us she

71

had lost all of her memory. It was Christmas 2000, and the family had gathered to celebrate. One of our sons had made a special gift for the family—a custom CD containing several songs by my father who had passed away two years before. Dad had recorded them while in his 20's and 30's—about fifty five years earlier, around the time when he and my mom were courting. The gift brought us all great joy, so we instantly popped it into the CD player. We wheeled Mom over near the speakers and turned it on. The moment his unmistakable tenor voice began to emerge from the speakers we saw Mom begin to stir in her wheel chair. Her dull eyes brightened and began to fill with tears. It seemed she was trying to touch him. Of course we all joined her in her weepy moment of reminiscence. While all other sensory stimuli had long ago ceased to have meaning to her, the sound of that special voice singing those familiar songs instantly retrieved the memories of her beloved. It seemed to us that for a blessed moment she was given a glimpse of the glory of her beloved's face.

Emotionally charged musical memories may be some of the most durable we possess. So use good music. Other suggestions to elicit emotion might include drama and video, elements of surprise, a touching testimony of God's grace, a poignant poem, etc.

3. What You Do First and Last

When our senses are bombarded with a great deal of information—such as happens when we attend an hour-long communion service—research indicates we tend to remember better what we hear first and last, often forgetting what comes in the middle. This phenomenon is referred to as the *primacy and recency effect*. This implies that how we begin the service is of utmost importance. In the language of preaching and teaching, our "hook" or introduction is key. We saw above how important attention is in choosing what will be discarded and what will be encoded into long term memory. If we don't grab their attention at the start, we may not have them throughout the rest of the time. An attention-grabbing hook should orient their minds to the direction the entire service will be going, and it will inform the "librarian in their minds" where to file the remainder of the incoming information.

Far too many preachers neglect their hook, and in so doing they waste much of the work they have done in preparing an excellent lesson. The audience never gets on board mentally, and few good memories are formed. The old saying still applies: it goes in one ear and out the other.

This principle also underscores how important it is for the service to climax in the eating of the bread and drinking of the cup. That final memory will linger, and that is the very thing which ultimately pictures Jesus.

4. Do it Often

Memory experts refer to the "distribution of practice effect." In layman's language, this means we remember better when we go over and over the same material. The principle is also dubbed "little and often." Learning anything is enhanced this way. We saw above that this actually physically strengthens the synaptic connections which store the memory. That's why we practice a musical instrument to learn how to play it better. That's why we review scriptures when we want to memorize them. The more we replay the memory and then correct it, the more accurate and durable it becomes. Why does one person forget his or her high school algebra and another doesn't? Likely because the first person never uses it again while the second person works as an engineer.

Jesus instructed us to observe the table regularly, and the "distribution of practice effect" also suggests that we do it often. As we do, we will continually reinforce accurate memories of Jesus and progressively correct inaccurate ones.

5. Correcting Inaccurate Memories

Some years ago while I was preaching my Sunday sermon, I told an illustration on myself. (It has always been my practice to be as transparent with my flock as possible so that they can be encouraged to see me also growing in the faith.) After the service my wife asked me if the story actually happened to me or to another person she named. I was taken aback. Then as I prayerfully sought God to know the truth, I realized that my mind had subtly exchanged a story I had read in a magazine about that other man and replaced it as my own personal experience. God's Spirit showed me I needed to deal with a subtle uprising of sinful pride. Telling that story had made me look good to my flock. The next Sunday I had to humbly stand before them and confess that I had lied. Interestingly, I later learned that this kind of thing is commonplace. Dr. Loftus' research has shown that our memory has what she calls a superiority complex and an egocentric complex which have "a way of making us think of ourselves in a gradually more and more favorable light."[70]

---

[70] Loftus, p. 141

A major endeavor of psychology today is devoted to understanding the pervasive effects of inaccurate memories. It is far beyond the scope of this book to discuss this matter in detail. It is, however, important to note that our natural capacity to remember—marvelous as it is—is seriously tainted. Its accuracy could be rated as falling somewhere along the scale between slightly biased to absolutely corrupted and laced with lies. We mentioned above how sin has darkened our carnal minds. The corrupting influences affect how we *interpret and select* the information which will be stored; they affect what *is* stored; and they affect how we *interpret and view* what is retrieved. C. S. Morgan said, "We fill up the lowlands of our memories from the highland of our imaginations."[71] Time also has a way of corrupting memories, causing them to get dusty and fuzzy.

The upshot of all of this is that we cannot always be sure a summoned memory is actually the truth. Much has been written concerning the emotional and spiritual consequences of corrupted memories. So for the purpose of this study, we need only to take note of two things: 1) the memories we have laid down about Jesus and His work of redemption may not be completely accurate, and 2) we may tend to forget our own sinfulness and need of redemption.

There is indeed wonderful news regarding our lamentable tendency to store inaccurate memories. First, our memories are malleable. In other words, they can be molded and changed and sent back to their storage locations with new, more accurate details. Secondly, the Word of God is specifically designed to bring truth into our minds and correct wrong ideas: "All Scripture is God-breathed and is useful for teaching, rebuking, *correcting* [italics mine] and training in righteousness, so that the servant of God may be thoroughly equipped for every good work" (2 Tim. 3:16-17). Therefore it must be our solemn mission to carefully and accurately present the truth of scripture each and every time we gather at the table. We must be vigilant to correctly present Jesus, and we must be cautious to allow our people to take an honest self assessment (as taught by Paul in 1 Cor. 11:28ff.). Dr. Loftus reminds us that "[p]eople tend to rewrite history more in line with what they think they ought to have done than with what they actually did."[72] The table should always fulfill this dual role, reminding us accurately of how sinful we were without Christ and how completely His death solved our problem.

A woman in my congregation shared with me that when she was younger she had had some rather frightening experiences at the Lord's table. Those expe-

---

[71] Quoted in Loftus
[72] Loftus, p. 142

riences had implanted some very wrong memories of the meaning of the Lord's table in her mind, causing her to cower in fear when she anticipated communion. As she attended the periodic communion services in our church, little by little she felt the truth setting her free. Over time she began to delight in assembling to remember Jesus. It was encouraging to hear her share deepened insights which came while worshipping at the table. Praise God, her memories were corrected by the Word of God.

6. Action is Vital

We noted in the last chapter that Jesus commanded us to *do* something when we gather to remember Him. Memory research confirms that this enhances our recall. It is said that we remember 10% of what we hear, 30% of what we hear and see, and 60% of what we hear, see and *do*. This is because "doing" invokes our motor skill memory which is much less subject to decay than our perceptual memory (e.g. we seldom forget how to ride a bicycle once we master it). Our motor skill memory is also available for recall without consciously trying to remember it. Further, "doing" reaches those folks among us who are the so-called "tactile learners" who are otherwise lost in a purely intellectual environment. So we are wise to seek avenues of "doing" in our communion services such as corporate singing and playing of musical instruments, quoting scripture aloud, passing the elements to one another, breaking off a piece of bread, holding the cup, writing down notes, following along in their Bibles, holding hands with their neighbors, raising their hands in worship, walking to a station to receive the elements, kneeling, etc. The more doing the better.

Sensational Gatherings at the Table

Our memory truly is sensational—pun intended. It is a most sensational gift of God, reflecting His very personhood, and it is also directly linked to our senses. In the last chapter we saw that the Lord's table is designed to evoke memories of Jesus which remind us of His beautiful person and His marvelous work of redemption. Now in this chapter we have seen that our senses were created to provide us with the data we need to create those memories. May God grant us the grace to make our gatherings at His table truly sensational.

In the next chapter we will turn our attention to enhancing the way learning happens when we gather to remember Jesus.

*　*　*　*　*

Chapter 6
Fertile Soil for Learning

Learning and Memory

Those who follow Jesus are called disciples. The Greek word behind *disciple* in the New Testament is *mathētēs* from the verb *to learn*. Thus, disciples are really learners. Jesus invited us to come to Him as learners: "Take my yoke upon you and learn from me, for I am gentle and humble in heart, and you will find rest for your souls" (Matt. 11:29).

Learning is a special kind of memory building. Memory is related to learning as knowledge is to wisdom. Learning applies what memory has stored. Learning renders memories accessible, meaningful, and *usable*. It is not enough to simply know God's truth and have it stored away in the recesses of our memories; we must put it to work in our lives. "The Bible was not written to satisfy your curiosity," says Howard Hendricks, "it was written to transform your life."[73] In chapter four we saw that a correct remembrance of Jesus at the table will induce a response of action towards the object of our remembrance. Hence we can see that learning is a key aspect of what it means to gather at the table in remembrance of Jesus.

From our earliest days we humans are learning; it's part of the grand design of life. It is fascinating to behold two-year-olds learning about the world around them. And how delightful to observe children acquiring skills in music and sports and reading. If we are good stewards of our minds and memories, we will be learning as long as our faculties allow.

We learn differently, though, as we grow from babes to adults. Paul describes this in 1 Cor. 13:11: "When I was a child, I talked like a child, I thought like a child, I reasoned like a child. When I became a man, I put the ways of childhood behind me." Jean Piaget, a Swiss psychologist, pioneered in the study of this phenomenon. His research, which has been widely confirmed, postulates that children's intellectual development passes through several stages. The beginning stages involve various degrees of concrete thinking.

---

[73] Howard G. Hendricks and William D. Hendricks, *Living by the Book*, Chicago: Moody Press, 1991, p. 284

We have all seen how abstractions elude us when we're very young. I will always remember the time my "preoperational"[74] daughter went to the store with her grandma. As she drove back into the driveway, Grandma miscalculated a distance and backed into a yard light Grandpa had carefully installed. As soon as she realized what she had done, with exasperation Grandma announced, "Grandpa's going to shoot me." A few minutes later, my daughter was asking Grandpa (an avid hunter) if he had a gun. "Of course I do, honey." "Oh, no!" exclaimed my daughter, horrified. "Please don't shoot Grandma!"

In God's good grace, we are enabled to mature past this very concrete stage of reasoning. Our minds become increasingly able to understand and apply concepts, to reason abstractly. In the Apostle Paul's terms, we "put childish ways behind us" somewhere in the pre-teen years. As adults, we are capable of thinking about the propositions presented to us in the Bible. Abstractions are seldom easy to apprehend, but they become entirely possible as our minds develop. Says Lee Edson:

> In the final period, from age 11 onward, the mind is liberated from that need for the concrete; it becomes capable of handling abstract concepts, hypotheses, theories. The teenager develops that uniquely human ability to think about thought.[75]

Learning by Analogy

A fact of great interest to us in this study of the Lord's table is that one of the most effective ways for us to apprehend and learn abstract concepts is to compare and contrast them to relevant analogues in the concrete world. The Creator has marvelously patterned the adult mind to be able to think about abstract concepts via analogy. In other words, even though adults may have matured past Piaget's stages of concrete-*only* thinking, we still utilize our concrete thinking to facilitate our abstract thinking. As we mentioned earlier, such reasoning proceeds from perception (sensory data from observations of the concrete world) to conception (abstract notions which actually exist only in the mind). Put yet another way, we more easily catch on to an abstract concept (i.e. learn it) when it is illustrated for us in the concrete world in which we live.

---

[74] Piaget's term for children between two and seven.
[75] Lee Edson, *How We Learn*, NY: Time-Life Books, 1975, p. 68

One reason for this is the manner in which memories are stored. Abstract ideas are encoded entirely into what is called semantic (verbal) memory. In contrast, concrete notions can be stored both semantically and visually, thus allowing them to have more retrieval tabs. For example, it is easier to re-member the word *tree* than the word *truth*, because the semantic concept in the letters t-r-e-e can be associated with the visual image of a tree. Truth, however, doesn't have a similar picture associated with it, unless we have filed away a mental image of some concrete situation in which truth exists. According to memory researchers Ellis and Hunt, "[C]oncrete words are bet-ter remembered than are abstract words."[76]

As a preacher, I am acutely aware of how this works in a sermon. It never ceases to amaze me how the audience lifts their eyes and scoots to the front of their seats when I say those magical words, "Let me illustrate" or "Let me tell you a story." I may be in the middle of presenting very Biblically sound exegesis and accurate exposition of the scriptures, but it's all abstractions un-til they can see it illustrated. As I tell the story I see light bulbs turning on in their heads. It's a wonderful thing to behold. The listeners are connecting the meaning of difficult abstractions to the world they know and perceive with their senses. The same holds true for illustrative visuals. Concrete analogies and illustrations enhance the ability of our people to learn the truth of God because they allow them to go back to the simpler reasoning of their "pre-operational" childhood days. The mental pictures acquired in this way can then be stored alongside the semantic concepts of the message.

I mentioned previously that the message of redemption which we celebrate at the table is a litany of abstractions: sin, judgment, spiritual death, God's love, forgiveness, substitutionary atonement, covenants, eternal life, truth, mercy, etc. How important it is for us, then, to help our people learn these blessed concepts by analogy! The Lord's table is uniquely fitted to help us do just that. Let me explain how.

Concrete Images of Abstract Eternal Truths

Life as we know it, according to the scriptures, exists in two dimensions. There is the physical life of the natural world (what the New Testament calls the *bios*) and the spiritual life of the heavenly, eternal world (called the *zōē*). I believe that God, the author of all life, saw fit to create one to be the mirror

---

[76] Henry C. Ellis and Reed Hunt, *Fundamentals of Human Memory and Cognition*, Dubuque, IA: Wm. C. Brown, 1983, p. 103

image of the other. Eternal life, with all of its amazing attributes and qualities, is an abstraction way beyond the understanding of our limited finite minds. But we are all very familiar with the finite realities of our time-space world. I have observed that the Creator marvelously instilled analogy after analogy into the workings of our physical life which, if we will notice them, powerfully furnish us with concrete mental pictures to help us learn the abstract semantic truths of redemption.

Numerous instances of this are found within the scriptures themselves. For example, Paul illustrates the abstract way that Christians are related to each other by comparing us to the human body (1 Cor. 12). He also compares the way our bodies will undergo resurrection after we die to the way a seed gives up its life to be transformed into the body of a new plant (1 Cor. 15). He illustrates the way mature believers encourage newer believers by describing the way real-life mothers and fathers care for their children (1 Thess. 2:7,11). Isaiah compares the abstract workings of the Word of God to the way water falls on the mountain tops and brings nourishing life to the valleys below (Isa. 55:10-11). The Psalmist compares his spiritual hunger to return to worship at the Temple to the way swallows return to their nesting places (Psa. 84:1-3). The Psalms also compare the way godly people grow in the realm of spiritual life to the way a tree grows in the natural world (Psa. 1:3).

Most of Jesus' parables are drawn from the natural world. In fact, the very word parable comes from *parabolē* which means "that which is thrown alongside." Thus a parable throws the concrete observation alongside of the abstract spiritual truth being considered. Jesus frequently invited His audience to look at nature and learn spiritual truth. For example, "Look at the birds of the air…. See how the flowers of the field grow" (Matt. 6:26-28).

Three Ways to Learn at the Lord's Table Via Analogy

Importantly, the Lord's table, with its sensory quality, provides us a unique and marvelous opportunity to expose our people to some of these analogies and help them learn about Jesus Christ and His redemption. Let's consider this under three categories.

1. Concrete Symbols and Images Built into the Lord's Table Itself

First, notice the elements themselves. The bread pictures Christ's body, an enormously complex abstraction. Yet, if we study the nature of bread, we gain much understanding of who Jesus is and what He does for us. Grain, which supernaturally springs from a seed sown into the earth, must be crushed and then subjected to high heat in order to make bread. Then it becomes the "staff of life" providing nourishment to the many cells of our bodies. The bread of the Passover was unleavened bread. Leaven is noted in the Bible as a picture of sin because of the way it spreads throughout the lump of dough. In addition, before the bread could picture Jesus' body, it had to be broken. The study of the communion loaf alone yields rich concrete images which facilitate much understanding of the complex spiritual abstraction of Christ's body.

The cup of wine or juice seals the New Covenant in Christ's blood. Again, the New Covenant is a complex series of abstractions involving Christ's offer of complete forgiveness for all sin through the sacrifice of the Lamb of God. If we will probe into the physical realm, we will gain much insight. We will need to look at the meaning of covenants in Bible times (including the marriage covenant which was sealed with a cup of wine), and especially the Mosaic Covenant. The physical imagery of Moses sprinkling cattle blood on the people as they stood before the base of a smoking mountain provides memorable and meaningful understanding of why Jesus' New Covenant was so significant. We also need to probe the Old Covenant practice of animal sacrifice. It is a graphic and sensory picture of the price God requires for sin. When we study animal sacrifice, we must not miss the many useful analogies offered by considering sheep, those most helpless—yet precious—creatures who illustrate both Jesus and us.

Of course, blood is a central object both in the Old and New Covenants, and the Lord's table is stained with it. As the scriptures say, the life is in the blood (Lev. 17:11), and when blood is shed, life comes to an end. We see astonishing parallels between the blood of Christ which brings life and purification to our souls and our own blood which supplies nourishment and cleansing to the cells of our body.[77]

---

[77] See an excellent treatment of this in Paul Brand and Phillip Yancey, *Fearfully and Wonderfully Made*, Grand Rapids, MI: Zondervan, 1987, and Paul Brand, *The Forever Feast*, (pub. data unknown) chapter 17.

The cup is filled with wine (or grape juice, depending upon your church tradition). The way grapes grow is a remarkable and graphic picture of spiritual growth (as described by Jesus in John 15), and the way grapes were crushed and fermented to produce wine is another striking picture of the life being taken from Jesus. Finally, the action of eating the bread and drinking the cup is a potent symbol of faith.

Thus, the simple communion elements themselves provide a wealth of opportunities to learn about Jesus through analogy. They supply a seemingly limitless array of visual, auditory, olfactory, tasting, and touching sensations to accompany the clear teaching of scriptural truths about the meaning of Jesus' death.

But beyond this there are all the associated sights and sounds of the matters and events surrounding Christ's suffering and death. The story of Christ's passion and crucifixion should stay fresh in every believer's mind because it is the very heart of the Gospel, and it is weighted down with sensory images which depict deep abstract redemptive truth. For example: We ask, "What is forgiveness?" Jesus answers by forgiving those who nailed Him to the cross. We ask, "What is love?" Jesus answers by remaining silent before His false accusers and accepting horrific suffering and death. We ask, "How bad is our sin?" Jesus answers by sweating blood in the Garden of Gethsemane while He begs God to remove the painful cup. Everything about Christ's crucifixion is graphic and sensory in the realm of *bios* life, and it all teaches powerful truth in the abstract realm of *zōē* life. For this reason, I have made it a practice to visually portray some aspect of the crucifixion every time we have gathered at the table.

Then consider the multitude of sensory images associated with the Passover. The Passover truly is one huge redemptive analogy. Powerful illustrations of spiritual truth were also conveyed whenever the disciples would gather around a table for a dinner that included the breaking of bread, a social custom laden with rich abstract and spiritual significance.[78] Also, when Jesus

---

[78] The Plymouth Brethren and other similar groups call their observance of the Lord's table *The Breaking of Bread*. That term was already prominent in Old Testament times to describe a memorial meal taken in community in honor of a deceased loved one (see e.g. Jer. 16:5-7). Breaking bread became particularly associated with Jesus because of His miracle of feeding the five thousand. In Luke's account (9:16) he says that Jesus blessed the loaves (aorist tense, *eulogēsen*), broke them (aorist tense, *kateklasen*), and then kept on giving (imperfect tense, *edidou*) the broken pieces to the crowd. This points to the wonderful reality that the bread of Jesus' body, once bro-

moved around that table washing the disciples' feet, He was dramatizing key redemptive truth traceable all the way back to Moses at the burning bush.[79]

To be sure, the Lord's table—even more than its predecessor the Passover—is also one huge redemptive analogy.

2. Concrete Illustrations from Typology and Jesus' Own Teaching

Now let's widen our field of view from the table itself to the Bible as a whole. We see redemptive types filling the Old Testament, and the Gospels are rich with the redemptive teaching of Jesus—especially His parables.

Let's observe Old Testament types[80] first. Many Bible students have noted the "scarlet thread of redemption" weaving its hopeful way through the pages of the Old Testament. From the moment of the fall in the Garden of Eden, God began to intentionally drop hints about His marvelous plan to redeem lost humanity through the death and resurrection of His Son. Those clues are styled in the shape of real life stories which show concrete illustrations of abstract redemptive truth. After announcing that He would send a Descendent of a woman to crush Satan (the beginning of the "messianic hope"), God clothed the sinful pair with animal skins (showing the necessity for innocent blood being shed to cover their spiritual nakedness). From that point on, we can trace the scarlet thread and messianic hope throughout the Old Testament. A few aspects of this are:

---

ken, is the very bread of life—and as such is able to keep on giving its life to us. The same combination of words and tenses appear later in Luke's account of Jesus with the couple from Emmaus (Luke 24:30). It's not surprising, then, that Luke would describe the early Christians' gatherings around the Lord's table *the breaking of bread* (Acts 2:42).

[79] The custom of foot washing was laden with redemptive images. It was a gesture of hospitality and honor to a guest, but it was deemed menial labor appropriate only for lowly servants. Feet got dirty in the dusty Middle East, and dirty feet (symbolic of sin) needed to be cleansed to facilitate intimate fellowship between host and guest. Taking off one's shoes was a gesture of respect towards the host. When Moses and others took off their shoes in the presence of Yahweh, it showed their humility and yet readiness to fellowship with God. When Jesus washed the disciples' feet He was demonstrating His desire for fellowship as well as modeling servanthood.

[80] In this book I use *type* in the theological sense of an Old Testament person or thing that represents a New Testament redemptive concept, particularly Jesus Himself. It is derived from Paul's usage of *tupos* in Rom. 5:14.

•<u>Noah's Ark</u> (Gen. 6-9)—The ark graphically portrays the consequences of sin and the fact that God's instrument of salvation must actually experience the battering of God's judgment for sin. It also shows that the way we receive this salvation is to enter God's chosen ark by faith.

•<u>Abraham Offering Isaac on Mt. Moriah</u> (Gen. 22)—This story vividly depicts the very abstract theological notion of substitutionary atonement: "God himself will provide the lamb for the burnt offering."

•<u>Joseph</u> (Gen. 37)—Joseph pictures Jesus because he was hated by his brothers and suffered death (in symbolism by being sold into slavery) and his father "saw the blood" of an innocent male goat. He was later exalted to a position of authority.

•<u>The Exodus</u>—Numerous aspects of redemptive typology are found in the story of the Exodus: e.g. the Israelites' hopeless slavery, their deliverance from death through faith via the blood of an innocent lamb displayed publicly on their doorposts, and their entrance into the promised land.

•<u>Rahab</u> (Josh. 2)—A woman who was openly known as a sinner displayed a scarlet cord to show her faith in the God of Israel. She was delivered when all those around her were judged and destroyed.

•<u>Crossing the Jordan</u> (Josh. 3)—The Jordan, like sin, separated the people from the promised land. The ark, like Christ, entered the river first and opened the way for all to pass across in faith.

•<u>Redemption of Animals</u> (Ex. 13:13, Numb. 18:15)—Unclean animals had to be redeemed by the sacrifice of an innocent clean animal, showing yet another example of substitution.

•<u>The Yearly Feasts</u> (Lev. 23)—Each of Israel's seven feasts pictures a facet of God's redemptive program. The feasts are filled with sensory stimuli that make the meaning exceedingly concrete and memorable. Yom Kippur (the Day of Atonement) is particularly poignant. It dramatizes the meaning of forgiveness with two goats: one is sacrificed to pay the price of sin, and one is sent away into the wilderness to show that the guilt of sin is gone.[81] It is important to note that Jesus quite literally fulfilled the four spring feasts when He died on Passover, lay buried during Unleavened Bread, rose on First Fruits, and sent the Holy Spirit on Pentecost. You will find a chart of the seven feasts in Appendix 2.

•Sacrificial System (Lev. 1-7)—The book of Hebrews makes it plain that Jesus fulfilled the types of the Old Testament sacrifices of bulls and goats. Thus, it is instructive for us to observe the manner in which animal sacrifice was conducted. The laws concerning sacrifice make it clear that the most important offerings (from God's viewpoint) were the voluntary love offerings which involved burning up the whole animal.[82] But before love offerings could be brought, sin offerings had to be made. This is a concrete picture of Paul's message in Rom. 12:1-2, and it is pertinent to the way we *come to the table* to remember the One Who is our sin offering, and then we *go from the table* to give our lives as voluntary burnt offerings of love.

•Tabernacle (Ex. 25-40)—The Tabernacle is a veritable treasure chest of redemptive typology; it is vivid, visual, concrete, and therefore memorable.

•Cleansing of Leprosy (Lev. 13-14)—Leprosy is a striking type of sin because not only was it miserable, but it also caused the victim to be shunned and excluded from the fellowship of the community. The elaborate ritual specified in the Mosaic Law for demonstrating cleansing from leprosy is replete with redemptive types: cedar wood, scarlet string, blood of a slain dove, hyssop, and the release of a live bird (akin to the release of the scapegoat on Yom Kippur).

•Moses and the Serpent in the Wilderness (Num. 21:4-9/ John 3:14-15)—The poisonous bite of a snake is a clear picture of sin, reminiscent of the serpent in the Garden of Eden. Lifting up the brass snake on the

---

[81] It is quite significant to note that the word describing the priest sending away the scapegoat in Lev. 16:21 (Heb. *shalach*) is translated by *aphiēmi* in the Septuagint. *Aphiēmi* is the common New Testament verb describing forgiveness, conveying the same notion of sending away the guilt and accountability for sin.

[82] We discern that the Whole Burnt Offering was the one most highly valued by God because it appears at the head of the list of offerings in Lev. 1.

pole is a picture of Jesus' crucifixion and death. The "healing look" is a clear visual of the abstract meaning of faith.

•Messianic Prophecies. Many Old Testament passages point to Jesus. Two are especially helpful at the Lord's table: Psalm 22 and Isa. 53. Psalm 22 furnishes astonishing details about Christ's crucifixion written a thousand years before Christ lived and nine hundred years before the Romans even invented crucifixion. Of course, Isa. 53 is the marvelous depiction of the suffering of the Lamb of God.

•OT Christophanies—Numerous times the invisible God made visible appearances in the Old Testament period. He appeared to Hagar (Gen. 16:7-13), Abraham (Gen. 22), Jacob (Gen. 31:11-13) and Gideon (Jud. 6:11ff) as the *Malach Yahweh* (Angel of the Lord); He appeared in the pillar of cloud and fire to the Israelites (Ex. 13:21, 14:19). He appeared as a "man" to Abraham and Sarah (Gen. 18), and He wrestled with Jacob (Gen. 32:24-30). He was visible to Moses and the seventy elders while they ate and drank (Ex. 24:9-11). He appeared as the Captain of the Lord's hosts to Joshua (Josh. 5:13-15), and He was seen in the fiery furnace with the three men (Dan. 3:25-28). Such visible appearances of the invisible God help us understand a great deal about who Jesus is, in view of His role as the visible member of the triune God.

•Many Other Characters can be studied as types of Christ, such as David, Joseph, Zerubbabel, and Melchizzedek. Note that Melchizzedek offered Abraham a meal of bread and wine (Gen. 14:18).

These examples should suffice to show how God planted a multitude of rich concrete images of Jesus and His redemption in the Old Testament. Each one offers great promise for bringing our people face to face with Jesus at the Lord's table through very memorable sensory images. I recommend taking advantage of a good book on Old Testament types, of which there are many.

Now let's turn our attention to the New Testament. It is also filled with scores of sharply focused redemptive pictures. Notice a few which are especially applicable for use around the Lord's table:

•The Lost Sheep, Lost Coin, and Lost Son (Luke 15)—These three stories are unmatched in their ability to connect with the experiences of our lives. They powerfully portray concrete images of our plight and the redemptive love of Jesus.

•The Four Soils (Matt. 13)—The way certain people respond to the gospel message is sometimes very hard to categorize and understand. It is indeed a confusing abstraction. However, Jesus gave us some very memorable visual images with the bird picking up the seed on the road, the seed dying quickly in shallow soil, the thorns choking out some plants, and the good soil producing a plentiful harvest.

•The "I Am's" of Jesus—John's Gospel records seven such utterances. Each one is worth devoting an entire communion service to its rich concrete redemptive images. ("I am... the bread of life; the light of the world; the resurrection and the life; the door; the good shepherd; the way, the truth and the life; the vine.") John also records several more "I Am's" in the Revelation (e.g. "I am... the alpha and omega, the first and the last, the root and offspring of David."). In fact, the vision of the glorified Christ in Revelation 1 could become a fertile series of communion messages with its rich similes and metaphors: white robe, golden girdle, white hair, eyes like fire, feet like burnished bronze, voice like the sound of many waters, etc.

•Bride/Bridegroom Metaphor—John 14 casts Jesus in the role of bridegroom going to prepare a home for His beloved bride, and then returning to catch her away. A number of other New Testament texts allude to this same imagery (e.g. the shout of the best man in 1 Thess. 4:16 and John 3:28-30). The ancient near eastern wedding customs provide an exceptionally vivid mental photo of the events surrounding Christ's second coming.

•Other Geographical, Cultural, and Historical Imagery—Much of the background to the New Testament story is laden with pregnant symbols. One can draw numerous redemptive parallels from studying such subjects as olives and olive trees, shoes and foot washing, the meaning of food throughout the Bible, wineskins, rocks, building methods, crowns (Jesus had to wear the crown of thorns before He could wear the crown of glory), etc.[83]

---

[83] Notice that one of the emblems of the curse in Eden was ground which produced thorns and thistles (Gen. 3:18). When God spoke to Moses from the burning

•<u>Stories From the Life of Christ with Redemptive Meaning</u>—Healing in the physical realm has direct parallels to healing in the spiritual realm, e.g. blindness, leprosy, paralysis, deafness, and even being raised from the dead. Certain teachings of Jesus draw attention to the meaning of forgiveness, such as Luke 7 and the woman taken in adultery (John 8). Some miracles also point to redemptive truth, such as the feeding of the five thousand and the calming of the storm on Lake Galilee.

I hope you agree that the New Testament overflows with vibrant concrete symbols of redemption which point us directly to a clearer understanding of who Jesus is and what He accomplished for us on the cross. When these illustrations are seen and heard around the table, they are powerfully effective in causing the eyes of our hearts to be enlightened in order that we "…may know the hope to which he has called you, the riches of his glorious inheritance in his holy people" (Eph. 1:18).

3. Concrete Illustrations from Science and Nature

We can also look directly at nature itself to gain marvelous insights into the workings of spiritual life. We must, however, exercise great caution here because the study of science and nature are not the study of God's written Word. On the other hand, if we believe that God is the author of all life, then we should feel liberty to search for illustrations in the natural world He created which illumine His spiritual truth. We must always remember to *teach* the written Word and *illustrate* it with the images of the natural world and not the other way around. A few examples will suffice to show the almost limitless buried treasure to be mined by the persistent observer of the natural world.

One of the most difficult abstractions Christians must grapple with is the question discussed by Paul in 1 Cor. 15: "How are the dead raised? With what kind of body will they come?" (1 Cor. 15:35). It is extremely difficult for us to grasp the transformation of these earthly bodies when we die. How does God work this process of "glorification?" Clearly God has planted an incredible illustration of this process right under our noses. It is seen in the metamorphosis of a butterfly. Take, for example, the exquisite monarch butterfly: In its first body, it lives a very limited existence as a caterpillar slowly crawling about milkweed plants, foraging on their leaves. Then comes the

---

bush, it was evidently a thorn bush (*batos*), implying that He was the God who was going to overcome the curse (Acts 7:30). Thus it was powerfully symbolic that Jesus wore the crown of thorns as He bore the brunt of the curse on the cross.

day when it "dies" and enters a cocoon. Once it enters this stage called the chrysalis, it completely turns into an amorphous liquid. The only remaining connection to its caterpillar past is its beating heart. Then comes the day when, within just a few hours, that liquid is most-amazingly transformed into a butterfly. Out it flies and begins to soar above where it once crawled. It will travel thousands of miles to the very tree in which its ancestors were born. We may not understand *how* God performs this miracle of metamorphosis, but the fact that it happens constantly all around us should give us hope that it is certainly no big deal for God to "…transform our lowly bodies so that they will be like his glorious body" (Phil. 3:21). Imagine how it would summon hope in your people if you showed PowerPoint slides or a video of a monarch's metamorphosis. It would truly encourage them to keep proclaiming the Lord's death until He comes (1 Cor. 11:26).

Water is another phenomenon of nature relating to the Lord's table. The way water behaves physically and chemically enables it to be the very stream of life itself. It carves pathways through resistant rock; it transports nutrients to living cells. It carries off waste products and is the very medium in which most of the biochemical processes of life occur. As far as we know, planet earth is unique in the universe for its rich treasure of water—both physical and spiritual. The One whom we remember at the table said He came to bring us His living water.

The way the human body works is, of course, an overflowing treasury of analogical truth. Many of our organs and systems illustrate aspects of redemption. For example the immune system provides rich concrete images of spiritual warfare: macrophages are white blood cells which gobble up bacteria, and natural killer cells spot and destroy cancerous cells. The blood itself is an amazing picture of nourishment and cleansing.

Other aspects of nature which exude sensory images of spiritual truths include light, the sun, the cycle of seasons, the growth of trees and flowers, the birth process, storms, bees, migration of birds and anadromous fish.

Of course, I have only scratched the surface of a very rich vein of gold. My intent is not to do your work for you, but to expose you to the wealth of opportunities which await you. If you will decide to expose your people's senses to concrete redemptive images at the table, this will provide fertile soil for them to learn more of who Jesus is and what He did for us. As an added bonus, I believe you will find yourself being thrilled as you gaze at these marvelous pictures of truth, and your enthusiasm will be infectiously evident at the table. Instead of merely going through the motions, telling them the dry abstractions of the Bible, you'll be sharing your personal discoveries of your own glimpses of Jesus' glory, and inviting them to join you. May your face shine like Moses' face shone every time he got a glimpse of God's glory.

Our next chapter explores the rich analogical and multisensory learning that was designed into the annual celebration of Israel's deliverance from Egypt, the Passover.

*   *   *   *   *

Chapter 7
Multisensory Roots

Nothing New

When Jesus lifted the bread and the cup in that Upper Room and said, "This is My Body... This is My Blood," He wasn't inventing something novel or unforeseen. It wasn't as though He suddenly dreamed up a clever new way to remember Him after He was gone. No, quite the opposite, indeed. He was actually fulfilling a prophetic type which had been preaching its multisensory message of remembrance for fourteen hundred years. Our brilliant Heavenly Father had crafted a phenomenally meaningful ceremony to commemorate Israel's miraculous deliverance from bondage in Egypt by the blood of the Passover lamb. He purposely loaded it with features that would provide the platform for Jesus to fulfill its types. The memory-making power of the Lord's table has tap roots deep in the soil of the ancient Passover ceremony.

That Little Word *This*

Since the Reformation, theologians have vehemently debated the meaning of the word *is* (*estin*) in the communion formula, and rightly so. Some believe that the bread actually becomes the body of Jesus because they fail to discern the metaphor implied in *is*. I have mentioned above that I stand with those who hold to the memorial supper view, meaning that *is* connotes *symbolizes* or *pictures*. To be sure, this is an essential point in a proper understanding of the Lord's table. However, I believe that it is equally vital to carefully notice the potent significance of the key word *this* (*touto*) in the communion formula.

When Jesus lifted the broken piece of unleavened bread before the eyes of His disciples and said "*This* is my body..." He was conveying much more meaning than simply singling out the piece of bread in His hand as distinct from all other pieces of bread. Of course it was that. More importantly, *this* points to what was going on in the room at that moment. Jesus and the Twelve were observing the time-honored inviolable sequence of the Seder as specified by Moses at the time of the first Passover in about 1400 BC and as refined by thoughtful rabbis through the following centuries. The particular piece of bread which He held in His hand as He said "*This* is My body" was the remaining piece of matzoh which had been broken before supper. In Seder symbolism, it had been broken, buried, resurrected, and was now being shared by all of the participants. The particular cup of wine which Jesus lifted and passed as He said "*This* is My Blood" was the third of four ceremonial cups, the one specifically called The Cup of Redemption by the rabbis. It was the cup of wine that most clearly pictured the blood of the Passover lamb. As Jesus uttered that little word *this*, it was as though He had become the ultimate interpretive guide to the true meaning of the Passover.

Since the Lord's table has roots deeply embedded in the Passover, one might think that a solid understanding of it would be considered essential for all those who participate in the Lord's table—and especially for those who lead it. But I have observed that many modern evangelical believers simply don't know about the Passover. To some, it's merely a great Old Testament story of God's rescue of Israel from Egyptian bondage. To others it's nothing more than the traditional springtime gathering of modern Jewish people who don't believe in Jesus. Far too often, I find few who are able to draw any meaningful connection between the Passover and the polished chrome communion set sitting prominently upon the hand-carved wooden table at the front of their sanctuaries displaying "In remembrance of Me."

The Whom and the What

Accordingly, in this chapter my desire is to describe the incredible value of this amazing ceremony. We will explore this on two levels. First, on the spiritual level, we will probe how Jesus fulfilled the typology of the Passover lamb when He became the Lamb of God Who takes away the sin of the world.[84] We will find that the Passover points to the One *whom* the table is all about. Then we will consider how the Passover is an exquisite example of ways to create deep and abiding memories of Jesus at the Lord's table. This drama repeatedly invokes all the senses and lays down deep, accurate, lasting, and retrievable redemption memories—which is *what* the table is all about. The Passover is a marvelous example of the concepts we have seen in the previous pages.

To this day, Jewish people relish their celebration of the Seder. Some time back, one of my university students informed me he would have to be absent for one week of class. He was planning to travel across the country to "do" the Passover with his wife's family. In that rather rigorous academic program, missing class meant an extra ten page paper, so students tried hard not to miss very often. Yet as this young man asked me for his make-up assignment, his face beamed with eager anticipation. He said he was happy to do the extra work just to be able to participate in the blessed event with the family.

---

[84] John 1:29

What is it that makes the Passover so exciting and *memorable*? We will seek to answer that question in this chapter and then challenge you to carry the impact of the memory-making power of the Passover into your modern observance of the Lord's Supper.

The Passover Points to Jesus

Only once in my ministry life have I had the privilege of discipling a young man who was raised in a Jewish home, but that experience is one I will never forget. David[85] went to synagogue school as a young boy and participated in all the rituals of devout Jewish people including the Passover/Seder. He met Jesus as his Messiah/savior while he served in the military. I met him shortly after his discharge, and I had the joyful privilege of helping him learn some of the basics of his new-found faith in Christ. Passover season was approaching, so I began to ask him about his experiences with the Seder. At first he was confused. Why would I, a Christian, be interested in his experiences with a Jewish ceremony? To him Passover was just a tradition that held no meaning other than a wonderful family bonding time and a sign of solidarity with other Jewish families. But I persisted, and so he began telling me all about the Seders he had done as a boy. As he went along, I began to point out the symbolism of various aspects of the ritual which he and his family had done together simply by rote so often. With his new eyes as a believer in Christ, for the first time he was enabled to comprehend the meaning of the symbols. He began to weep and shout and pound the table all at the same time! He was blown away as he saw picture after picture of Jesus and His redemption. I will always cherish that day. I realize now that I was permitted to witness a dazzling moment of divine revelation. The Holy Spirit caused David to see vivid pictures of Jesus emerging from memories of his early experiences with the Passover. Such is the memory-making power of the Passover.

Peter and John's Witness

No one knew more clearly that the Passover points to Christ than the early disciples who actually took the dinner with Him the night before He died. Let's focus in on two of them in particular, Peter and John. Both of them were radically impacted by the events of their last Passover with Jesus. Evidence of this shows up in what they later preached and wrote—particularly in two themes that surface in their writings. Notice how they speak about "the lamb" and "the blood":

---

[85] Not his real name

93

<u>Peter</u>: "For you know that it was not with perishable things such as silver or gold that you were redeemed from the empty way of life handed down to you from your ancestors, but with the precious blood of Christ, a lamb without blemish or defect" (1 Pet. 1:18-19).

<u>John</u>: "Then I saw a Lamb, looking as if it had been slain, standing at the center of the throne, encircled by the four living creatures and the elders…. And [the worshippers] sang a new song, saying: 'You are worthy to take the scroll and to open its seals, because you were slain, and with your blood you purchased for God persons from every tribe and language and people and nation.'" Revelation 5:6-9).

Where did they get this emphasis on Jesus as the Lamb Who redeemed us with His blood? Is it possible the Holy Spirit enabled them to put two and two together after doing the Passover with Jesus the night before He died? Let's notice an interesting detail about the hands-on Passover they took together. Jesus gave orders to the disciples to find an Upper Room He had prearranged, and He instructed these two men, Peter and John, to prepare the Passover.[86] That technical language meant that they had to go out into the marketplace and buy an innocent unblemished lamb[87] and then take it to the Temple for slaughter. There, amid thousands of others who were also leading innocent lambs to the slaughter, they watched while the priest sliced its throat, caught the spurting blood in a bowl, and then poured it out around the altar. I imagine them pulling their outer garment over their mouths as they winced in pain as the blood gushed from the spurting jugular. I seriously doubt it was *ever* easy to witness this tragic spectacle.

Then, after leaving the Temple compound, they carried that dead lamb's body back to the house to gut it, skin it, and prepare it to be cooked. A cooking fire was built, and the lamb placed over it to roast until it was ready for the dinner. Before dinner had even *started*, these two men had already personally witnessed the bloody scene of an innocent Passover lamb pouring out its life, and then being judged with the hot coals of the cooking fire.

But it wasn't over. During the dinner, all the symbols of that ancient ritual pummeled their senses—the raucous blast of the ram's horn trumpet, the pungent herbs, the roasted meat, the unleavened bread, the blood red wine,

---

[86] Luke 22:8 in Greek: "Prepare the paschal [lamb] for us so that we may eat [it]."

[87] This is a guess. It is possible the disciples had already selected and purchased the lamb a few days earlier on the 10th of Nisan as most of the Jews had done in keeping with Ex. 12:3. But I conjecture that it would have been unwieldy for the itinerant disciples to travel for five days with a lamb.

the flickering candles, the cool water being applied to their dirty feet by their beloved Lord, etc. Their ears heard Jesus say "This is My body" and "This is My blood." Their eyes saw the bread and cup. Their mouths tasted that bland unleavened bread and the heady aromatic wine. Their hands held the various items as they were passed around the table. All the while they were being bathed in the warmth of the One Who was "loving them to the very end."[88] That last Passover with Jesus must have left those men's minds and hearts exploding from sensory overload.[89] And they had heard Him forcefully identify Himself as the very fulfillment of the symbolism towards which the Passover pointed.

So as they left the Upper Room that night, the Passover ceremony may have been finished, but it wasn't really over yet. In fact, the horrific cascade of sensory events we call the Passion and Death of Christ were just beginning. What followed was a night and day of agony and terror. It all culminated with Jesus hanging on the cross, the innocent victim of Jewish deceit and Roman brutality. It's not certain just where Peter was during the crucifixion, but he declared himself to be a witness of the crucifixion.[90] And we *are* told that John watched the execution from the very foot of the cross.[91] So both of these men had first hand knowledge of how Jesus had died innocently and poured out His blood on the cross. To them it must have been surreal; it must have seemed like déjà vu—like they were living out the Passover in real life which they had just enacted in symbolism the night before. Once the resurrected Christ took them aside and opened their minds, they were supernaturally enabled to completely put the whole puzzle together.[92] What emerged in their minds, hearts, preaching, and writing was a graphic picture of Jesus, the Lamb of God, whose innocent blood was poured out to pay for the sins of all people. To Peter and John, and likely the other early apostles as well, the Passover lamb was clearly a type of the coming Savior. Jesus was undeniably the fulfillment of that type.

Let us also not forget the exquisite timing of these events: Jesus was presented on the donkey on the 10th of Nisan—the very day thousands of families

---

[88] *Eis telos ēgapēsen autous* (John 13:1)

[89] It is interesting to consider John's words in 1 John 1:1 in this context of the multisensory Passover: "That which was from the beginning, which we have heard, which we have seen with our eyes, which we have looked at and our hands have touched—this we proclaim concerning the Word of life."

[90] Acts 3:15, 1 Pet. 5:1

[91] John 19:26, 35

[92] Luke 24:44-48

were selecting and purchasing their lambs.[93] He celebrated the Passover with His Galilean disciples on Thursday, the very day Galilean rabbis had specified as their 14th of Nisan. He died on Friday, the day that Judean rabbis had specified as their 14th of Nisan according to their slightly different determination of the date of the full moon. In other words, He was able to take the Passover and be the Passover on the precise days specified by Moses in Exodus 12. It is no wonder, then, that Paul flatly declares, "Christ our Passover lamb has been sacrificed."[94]

This typological correspondence is highlighted in the explanation of the symbols in the Seder ceremony included as an appendix to this book.

The Quintessential Memory Maker

The Passover—as it was celebrated by Jesus with His disciples in the Upper Room—was a composite service which had evolved through the enlightened additions by thoughtful rabbis during the fourteen hundred years between the time of Moses and the time of Christ. The original ceremony was a very simple dinner of roasted lamb and unleavened bread "upon" bitter herbs.[95] It is especially important to notice that the basic structure and purpose of the Passover were not human inventions. Moses simply reported what God had revealed to him and Aaron.[96] Later rabbinic embellishments simply added dimensions of richness to the divine original. The first Passover was the last of the ten plagues which finally moved Pharaoh to release the Israelites and allow them to embark on their journey to the promised land. Yet it was far more than one of the ten plagues. In the later formulations of the Levitical calendar, the Passover marked the beginning of the Jewish year. It was the first of the seven feasts comprising the Jewish religious year.[97] If we examine the typological meaning of these seven feasts we quickly see that God's entire plan of redemption in Christ was enacted in the symbols of these seven feasts. (See Appendix 2.)

It is crucial to notice why God instituted the annual observance of the Passover in their homes on the night of the first full moon of spring. It was so that parents could teach their children to *remember* their deliverance from

---

[93] Ex. 12:3
[94] 1 Cor. 5:7
[95] Hebrew text of Ex. 12:8
[96] Ex. 12:1
[97] Lev. 23

bondage in Egypt by the blood of an innocent lamb.[98] In fact Moses says, "And it will be like a sign on your hand and a symbol on your forehead that the LORD brought us out of Egypt with his mighty hand."[99] God did not want them to forget their redemption, so He designed a very visual and very palpable memory-maker. Later rabbis named the ceremony "The Haggadah" which is from the Hebrew verb *nagad* meaning "to tell" or "show forth."[100] They derived this from Ex. 13:8 where the text says, "On that day tell your son…." Interestingly, few participants would ever say they *heard* or *watched* a Passover; they would be much more likely to say they *did* a Passover. The telling of the Passover story is in the doing of the Passover actions. Modern educators might say that the Passover was aimed at the tactile learners in the class.

Now this synesthetic reminder of His redemption was only part of His larger scheme of structuring mnemonic devices into the lives of His people. From the earliest days of creation, God began to reveal Himself in two very special ways: first as our Creator, and then as our Redeemer. On day four of creation, the account says that He made the two great lights, the sun and the moon, to "…serve as signs to mark sacred times, and days and years."[101] He established a 7-day week (determined by the time marker, the sun) with a special rest on the seventh day to perpetually remind us that He made us. The 7-day week truly is God's mnemonic device to constantly cause us to remember that "it is he that hath made us and not we ourselves."[102] The proper observance of the Sabbath is designed to evoke sweet memories of our Creator.[103]

God also established a 7-feast year (determined by the time marker, the moon) to constantly remind His people that He is our Redeemer. Passover stands at the head of these seven feasts and is the one that dramatically pictures the necessity of blood to accomplish redemption. A cursory glance at the seven feasts shows their wonderful typical meaning. It is beyond the scope of this book to examine these feasts in depth, but the point we need to glean here is that God intentionally planted exceptionally sensory-rich rituals

---

[98] Ex. 12:24-27

[99] Ex. 13:16

[100] It is likely that Paul was alluding to the *Haggadah* when he said, "For whenever you eat this bread and drink this cup, you proclaim (*katangellō*) the Lord's death until He comes," 1 Cor. 11:26).

[101] Gen. 1:14

[102] Psa. 100:3, KJV

[103] Ex. 31:17

into the life of His people to act as memory goads—constantly reminding them that He was their Redeemer.

It was impossible to observe these feasts without involving most or all of the senses and experiencing significant emotions in the process. Imagine the unforgettable chill that would run through your body at sundown on the day the moon became dark in September[104] as dozens of priests would start blowing shrill blasts on their shofars to signal the beginning of the autumn festival. Those fall feasts were particularly poignant in juxtaposing the pathos of the mournful Day of Atonement against the joyful dancing and celebrating of Booths. To observe the seven feasts was to intertwine body, mind, and spirit in a focused celebration of the Redeemer. The feasts came around *every year*. So the memories became deeply encoded—since they were reviewed, repeated, reinforced and laid down with a myriad of synesthetic retrieval cues.

Yet another aspect of the Passover was woven into the fabric of Jewish life from Moses to Jesus and also served to graphically and dramatically picture their redemption while serving as a mnemonic device. It was the redemption of the firstborn taught in Exodus 13. Every time a firstborn male person or animal was born into a Hebrew home, the people were instructed to offer a sacrifice in its place. This is the rite Mary and Joseph were performing when Simeon recognized the baby as the long awaited Messiah.[105] God allowed millions upon millions of innocent animals to perish in generation after generation in order to spark curiosity in the children. This would then open the door for parents to commemorate their redemption by explaining the Passover.[106]

The One who created the human capacity for memory—and is therefore intimately acquainted with how memory works—carefully crafted rites and rituals to resonate with the way He designed memory. To use a computer analogy: The one who made the hardware also wrote optimal software.

---

[104] In ancient Jewish reckoning, the dark of the moon near the autumnal equinox was the first day of Tishri.

[105] Luke 2:22-24

[106] Ex. 13:12-16

Emblems of the Great Drama of Redemption

Now let's look at some of the essential elements of the Passover in existence at the time Jesus hosted the Seder in the Upper Room. Each piece of the ritual virtually drips with the sweet honey of redemptive analogy. The Hebrew word *seder* means "order," and it is used to describe the specified content and order of events constituting an official Passover observance. As mentioned above, the first Passover was elegant in its simplicity. Later additions only enhanced its capacity to "tell" the message of redemption.

The setting of the Passover is the time when the Children of Israel were in bondage to Pharaoh and had to make bricks for His extravagant building projects. They were languishing in their bondage and had no way to free themselves. Their plight seemed hopeless. Students of scripture are well aware that Egypt is often viewed as a symbol of sin's pleasures, idolatry, and Satan's bondage. Interestingly, John (the apostle of the blood and the lamb) refers to Jesus as being figuratively crucified in Egypt.[107] Symbols of Egypt's bondage appear in the Seder in the bitter herbs which are taken with salt water (picturing tears) and in the *charoseth* (a mixture of applesauce, raisins and nuts) which pictures the bricks and mortar. The ten plagues are rehearsed during the Seder, and participants dramatize their awe-inducing demonstration of God's redemptive power by banging their forks on their plates or acting out the disgusting nature of each one. It is not a distant reach to compare the setting of the Passover with our present day plight in sin.

The Hebrew name for Passover is *pesach*, and it is transliterated into Greek as *pascha*). It means just what the name implies: "to skip over, to hop over, to pass over." The name is derived from the original story when the death angel spared the firstborn sons in the homes adorned with the atoning blood of a perfect, male, innocent lamb. Killing the firstborn sons was emblematic of the whole group. They were all worthy of death. Again, we see the parallel in Christ's redemption. As Paul reminds us, "all have sinned and fall short of the glory of God" and are worthy of the wages of death.[108] Peter reminds us that Jesus was an innocent lamb without blemish.[109]

---

[107] Revelation 11:8
[108] Rom. 6:23, 3:23
[109] 1 Pet. 1:18-19

At the first Passover, each household was instructed to slay its own lamb and then paint the blood on the exterior face of the door frame of their house.[110] It was a rather bold public proclamation of the family's faith in the power of the lamb's blood to somehow deliver from death. They were instructed to use a bunch of hyssop as a paint brush. Hyssop is a consistent type of public appropriation of cleansing from sin.[111]

As you work through the Seder Jesus took with His disciples—and the Seder you can take with your church and/or family (see Appendix)—you will behold a wealth of redemptive analogies: Emblems of sin and bondage (bitter herbs, *charoseth*, and the plagues), emblems of redemption (roasted lamb, unleavened bread, covenants sealed in wine), and emblems of hope: the joyful singing and dancing that follow the dinner. You will also find all the senses stimulated: the smell of roasting lamb, the taste of bitter herbs, the sight of flickering candles in the festive room, the sounds of heart-felt prayers, the feel of washing your hands in cool water, and much more. You will see learning take place through question and answer, through story telling, through reading scripture, through repetition, and through tactile action, and fun—all in community. Most of all, you will see Jesus.

What Should I Do with the Passover?

Since the Lord's table has roots which penetrate so deeply into the fertile soil of the Passover, it should be apparent that it would be extremely valuable to do a Passover with your family and/or church. I encourage you to consider the example I have provided as an appendix to this book.

Compare your experience at the Lord's table in your present church setting to the rich multi-sensory experience of the Passover. Do you and your congregation anticipate the table like my student anticipated the Passover with his family? Do you develop and reinforce compelling images of Jesus from the pregnant analogies of His life and death? Do you spend the amount of time with the table that was spent around the Seder table? Does your experience at the table reach your memory via all the senses—repeatedly, analogically and with significant emotional components?

---

[110] Ex. 12:22
[111] Lev. 14:6, Psa. 51:7

If you are able to answer "Yes," I suspect the memory banks of your mind and heart are packed with glistening glimpses of the glory of Jesus and you have come to love and serve Him with an unquenchable passion. I suspect your flock cannot wait for the next time you announce that the service will be devoted to cultivating further memories of our glorious Jesus through His table. They might even change their vacation plans to be there. I suspect you have a growing group of disciples who are passionately in love with Jesus and are increasing in their ability to share that love with others because of their abiding intimacy with their Lord. Oh, I pray there may be more like you.

But I suspect many of you have to honestly say your experience with the Lord's table bears little resemblance to the Passover. If you had to prove in court that your observance of communion was rooted in the Passover, you would lose your case for lack of evidence. Your current dull and dry experience may be sad testimony to the commonly held theological viewpoint teaching that the Passover was part of the Old Covenant, and as such, it passed away when the New Covenant was instituted. Of course, there was a huge shift from the Old to the New, but the way we encode and recall memories hasn't changed. Accordingly, we would be foolish to abandon the divinely inspired methods God crafted to beautifully mesh with the way He made our memory. Remember the hardware/software analogy above? When we abandon the teaching patterns taught by the Passover, we have trashed the software.

Two important action steps emerge from this mnemonic consideration of the Passover. First, because of its beauty and lavish pictures of Jesus, why not consider learning and celebrating Passover (a Christian version, of course) with your family and/or congregation? I recommend you use it to replace some of the pagan fertility rites which have hijacked our spring observance of the Passion and Resurrection of Jesus. Fewer eggs, bunnies, and Easter,[112] and more lamb, bitter herbs, unleavened bread, and fruit of the vine. The Passover/Resurrection Dinner which I have given you in the Appendix was developed for my family. The impetus for writing it came from the day I walked outside my house and saw my children searching for eggs and bunnies to celebrate the resurrection of Jesus. Something was terribly wrong with that picture, and so from that year onward it became our annual spring tradi-

---

[112] Eggs and bunnies are well known pagan symbols of fertility. Eastre was the Anglo-Saxon pagan goddess of spring (on a par with the Egyptian Isis, Phoenician Ishtar, and Canaanite Ashtarte).

tion to celebrate the Passover.[113] I have come to love it; it has helped me and many others develop precious memories of Jesus. I encourage you to give it a try. I think you and your flock will be blessed.

Second, learn from the way the Passover teaches about Jesus via the senses, emotions, analogies, and hands-on action. Bring these methods into your regular observance of the Lord's table. If your recent excursions to the Lord's table have been languishing in the doldrums, I pray that you will revitalize them with the warm winds blowing from the Passover.

*   *   *   *   *

---

[113] The dilution of Passover and its syncretization with paganism is not new. The men who translated the King James version of the Bible in 1611 translated the word *pascha* with *Easter* at Acts 12:4.

Chapter 8

A New Priority

If you have decided to join me in this zeal to adopt a new model and bring your people's senses fully into contact with the power of the table, you will have to pay the price. So let's count the cost. What will be required if you make this decision? I'd like to suggest ten important things that should accompany your decision to make the table a priority so that you can effectively exploit its wonderful memory-making potential.

1. Passionate Leadership

First and foremost, you, the leader, must be deeply in love with Jesus, the focus of the table. I assume you are, else you wouldn't have read this far. As you, yourself, gain glimpses of Jesus' matchless glory, you will find yourself becoming more and more like the prophet Isaiah who, according to John, "…saw Jesus' glory and spoke about him" (John 12:41). In addition, I pray you will also fall deeply in love with the table itself, seeing it as a gold mine brimming with nuggets glistening with glimpses of His glory. When you do, you will not be able to restrain yourself from talking about it with genuine excitement. You will long for the table when it is coming, and you will enter into its fullness when it is present. Your excitement for communion will be the pace setter. Your flock will see what you see; they will hear what you hear; they will feel what you feel. Your passion will be the divine spark which kindles the blaze in the hearts of your flock. On your shoulders, they will be lifted a little closer to His glory.

If your personal study has touched you deeply, you will find yourself standing on holy ground as you lead the Eucharist. Holy ground has a way of causing God's people to take off their shoes.

2. A Clearly Defined Goal

Every time you lead a service around the table, I believe you should pointedly ask the group, "Why are we here?" And the answer should clearly resound every time: "To remember Jesus." This is the goal; there is no other. It's all about *Him*. Further, I believe you should say something like: "What I want to share with you today is designed to create a fresh and vivid picture of Jesus in your heart and mind, so that you can love Him more deeply and serve Him more fully." Then you must keep this goal in your mind constantly as you prepare the service, and—even more importantly—as you lead it. All the spokes of the wheel should point towards this hub.

3. A Single-Purpose Service

The old model was a tacked-on, get-it-over-quick addition to an otherwise full service. A new model means that we devote the entire service to the table. We give it top priority by building all the elements of the service—like the spokes just mentioned—around the theme to be taught at the table. We announce the table well in advance so the participants can adequately prepare their hearts and minds. The sermon on this occasion is an aspect of teaching pointing to Jesus. The music, scripture reading, visuals, and even the very ambiance of the room (such as banners, unique seating around the table, etc.) all point to Jesus. Of course, the table itself commands preeminence. I have found lowered lighting with a spotlight on the table adds significant atmosphere, somewhat reminiscent of the prominence of the Seder table.

Of course this means it needs to be OK to stop whatever other teaching series we might be engaged in to celebrate the table and remember Jesus. It is imperative we don't view this as an interruption in our teaching. Quite the opposite: We must view it *as the very best of our teaching.*

4. Thorough Preparation

Whereas the old model required zero preparation, a new model requires substantial preparation. As in much of life's endeavors, the famous peanut machine principle I learned from my seminary professor, Dr. Howard Hendricks, applies: what you put in determines what you get out. If you want maximum impact, you must devote maximum effort to excellent preparation.

This begins with good ideas. Fortunately, the scriptures are all about Jesus. He is seen on every page of the New Testament and most of the pages of the Old. He is also seen in the majesty of His creation. So there is no shortage of wonderful glimpses of His glory. I made it my practice to keep a file of communion service ideas. As you read the scriptures or other commentaries, jot down subjects or ideas that come to your attention. For example, I'll never forget the time I was reading in Genesis about Melchizzedek, and I noticed that He offered bread and wine to Abraham. This started a wonderful path of study about this early type of Christ and the table. As I observed nature and matters of science and I saw the correlation with some aspect of the person or work of Christ, I would also jot them down in the file. I remember reading an article about the physiological cleansing and protective qualities of blood. Suffice it to say, not long after that, we were gathered around the table looking at pictures of red and white blood cells and marveling at the cleansing power of Jesus' blood.

Ask God to make your eyes alert to spot redemptive analogies and pictures of Jesus as you read the Word. Not long ago I was reading Stephen's speech in Acts 7 just before he was martyred. For some reason I had never before noticed that the burning bush which Moses encountered was actually a *thorn* bush. That started a long, rich trail of study that ended in a New Year's Eve communion service showing why Jesus *had* to wear a crown of thorns in order to conquer the curse for us.

It's good to let ideas prayerfully percolate. I find that God will frequently bring resources and experiences into my life when I'm thinking about a future topic for teaching. He will help me find illustrative material and collaborative resources. This requires time. The kind of teaching I am advocating cannot be prepared late on Saturday night.

Then comes solid study and proper exegesis of the scriptures. We are enjoined to "rightly divide the Word of God"[114] whenever we approach it, and this should never diminish, especially when our study involves Jesus and those many types and analogies which point to Him. As I prepare, I try to keep Jesus' words to Peter in the back of my mind: "Do you love Me?... feed my lambs."[115] Nourishing food for the flock grows in the rich soil of the rigorous exegetical work of the shepherd. This assumes your study encompasses careful linguistic and grammatical analysis as well as pertinent historical, geographical and cultural background material. If the goal is to present accurate glimpses of Jesus' glory as presented in the Biblical record, then the means to reaching that goal demand accurate exegesis and hermeneutics.

5. Teamwork

The sooner you learn that you were not given all the spiritual gifts, the sooner your ministry of the table will flourish. You may be a very gifted "mouth,"

---

[114] 2 Tim. 2:15, KJV
[115] John 21:15. Note Ezekiel's caution to shepherds in Ezek. 34:2-10.

but a mouth is pretty dysfunctional without the rest of the body.[116] Your flock is a gifted group. They will be honored and blessed if you draw them into your circle of ministry around the table, and you will be far more effective in accomplishing the goal. So build a team.

Your team can include people gifted in art and other forms of visual communication, people who do drama and poetry, musicians and singers, technically minded people who know how to utilize the latest technology for audiovisuals, people who know how to create a mood with decorations and lighting, people who prepare the elements (i.e. bread and cup) and display them with flare, people who do the service-work of moving chairs and tables around, and—most importantly—people who can supply ideas to help you expand your communication ability far beyond the limitations of your own world.

I remember the time I was planning to lead a Lord's table service around the theme of Jesus in the Garden of Gethsemane. In the course of life, I just "happened" to hear one of our musicians play and sing an old song called "'Neath the Old Olive Tree." I quickly went to her and asked her to prepare that song so that it could figure prominently into the middle of our teaching on Jesus in the Garden. It was of the gospel/folk genre, and turned out to be a wonderful feature of that service. Her music spoke far more to the hearts of the flock than I could have ever said with my mouth.

Consider how much more impact you would have when you teach about the cleansing power of blood if you actually had a doctor or nurse demonstrate it. Every person in the room understood when I had a nurse pump up a blood pressure cuff on a volunteer's arm and then just leave it for a minute or so. As the volunteer began to cry out in pain, it became obvious how our blood is constantly cleansing and feeding the cells.

I have found it extremely helpful to gather a team to assist in evaluating and developing my embryonic ideas about a particular theme that I would like to teach. I like to have representation from several sectors of the congregation: older, younger, musical, dramatic, cerebral, emotional, etc. It is good to let your team help you evaluate your ideas in terms of how they will impact the visual learners, the tactile learners, the thinkers, the feelers, etc. Whether you know it or not, we wear blinders to the way others think and learn. The more you can allow your ideas to percolate through the viewpoints of others, the

---

[116] See 1 Cor. 12:17.

more effective will be your presentation in touching more of the flock with your message. Let them offer ideas and then carry them out.

The communal aspect of the table is taught by Paul in 1 Corinthians 10:17: "Because there is one loaf, we, who are many, are one body, for we all share the one loaf." And it is reiterated in 1 Cor. 11:33: "So then, my brothers and sisters, when you gather to eat [at the Lord's table], you should all eat together." When we work as a team in preparing the table—and we work as team in observing the table—we model this wonderful theological truth.

6. Creativity

The team will jar you loose from your deeply entrenched rut of simply talking when you preach and teach. They will help you develop creativity. A new model of the Lord's table demands it. If you are going to choose this fresh path of invigorating the memory through the senses and emotions, you must opt to break out of that well-worn rut. If you find it hard to do so, then depend upon the creativity of your team.

We never choose creativity because it's novel and impressive and draws attention to itself. Rather, we choose creativity because it reaches the hearts of our audience with the message we intend. Every time our flock gathers we are battling the "Pavlov's dog effect." If they have grown accustomed to a predictable habit of presentation, there is a significant chance that they might never see Jesus. But a creative approach can awaken them from that mental drowsiness and bring the message home with great impact.

Keep in mind that the generation to which we minister is a thoroughly visual generation. Like fish, we swim in an ocean of images welling up from the ubiquitous springs of technology and media which define the twenty first century. Visual technology has indelibly shaped the minds of our audience. If we don't use videos, PowerPoint, drama, and well-placed visual objects, we will be unable to speak the language of our people. One of the great resources available to us today is the wealth of videos that are being produced by gifted video communicators. Your team should be taking advantage of these resources.

A key goal of our creativity must be to find modes of expression which touch the various senses with compelling images of Jesus and attach an emotional component to the cerebral message. Of course, each teaching theme will encompass its own unique set of possibilities. The goal will always be to enrich the presentation with memory cues which go beyond the mere verbal presentation of the message. The more the better. The happy marriage of solid Biblical exegesis and creative modes of expression breeds the marvelous offspring called clear communication of the truth.

7. Exalting Jesus

It should go without saying… but I'm going to say it anyway: Exalt Jesus in everything you do and say. Throughout the service, keep a bright spotlight shining on Jesus—it's all about Him. He said, "I, when I am lifted up from the earth, will draw all people to myself."[117] Sometimes, when teachers decide to become creative, the cart gets out ahead of the horse, and the creative modes of expressions *themselves* steal the spotlight. We must never forget that we are attempting to carry out His call to "remember Me."

I consider communion Sunday one of my most important times to teach about Jesus. On other days I am teaching about the whole counsel of God. But around the table, all eyes are fixed on Jesus. We must give our best energy to keep Him central and exalt His majesty. I like to lead the entire service standing at the table with the elements spotlighted in front of me. At appropriate moments during the service I will gesture towards the elements to provide a visual cue that what we are doing is pointing to Jesus.

8. Opening a Window

Here is the genius of a new model: Each time we gather, we open one window through which we gaze at Jesus. Sometimes I will actually say, "As you look at the bread and cup displayed on this table today, I want to ask you to think of them as a window through which you can see a very special picture of your precious Lord and Savior." One time it may be looking through the window of His beautiful hands (as in Appendix 3), another time it might be the window of the bronze serpent in the wilderness, and another time it could be one of the "I Am's" of John. But each time it is a single window which we open and then strain our senses to see and hear and feel Jesus. In this model, the entire service coheres around a single aspect of the revelation of Jesus Christ which is presented to all of the senses. Then the service climaxes in the tasting of the bread and wine and seeing a memorable picture of the Redeemer in the mind's eye. As the leader of this service, think of your-

---

[117] John 12:32

self as a person pulling back the curtains on a window through which are exhibited the glories of Jesus.

9. Appropriate Timing

Who came up with the plan to observe the Lord's table strictly on the first Sunday of the month, anyway? Certainly there is nothing inherently wrong with this tradition, but in my opinion this first-Sunday custom is one of the factors contributing to the Pavlovian lethargy which dogs the old model. The table's predecessor was an annual event. However, Paul's report of Jesus' own instructions open the door to considerable latitude in the timing and spacing of our observance of the table. He says, "Do this *as often as* you do it,"[118] so we are free to do what works best in our own unique cultural setting. "As often as we are willing to remember and to proclaim the death of Christ, we will celebrate Communion."[119] Early church father, Ignatius, encouraged us to celebrate the Eucharist frequently.[120] I personally apply this to mean I can share the Lord's table with a small group when it seems appropriate. I can celebrate it with my spouse or family when it seems appropriate, and we should take it together as a corporate body as often as it fits within our larger purposes of leading our flocks to good pasture. I am aware of a church which has incorporated the bread and cup into the fabric of their worship time *every week* during a series of lessons on living in light of God's grace.

In the corporate setting, my pastoral experience offers the following suggestion: The model we are describing in this book seems to work well about every seven weeks. Seven is the number of a completed cycle in scripture. Seven weeks gives you sufficient time to thoroughly prepare your service as we have described above. This interval is often enough to keep the memory of Christ's death fresh, while not being too often for it to become rote or shallow or commonplace.

We can also designate communion Sunday to fall on various occasions when it seems appropriate. I remember a Christmas communion where we com-

---

[118] Literal translation of *hosakis ean*, 1 Cor. 11:26. See a similar usage of this phrase in Revelation 11:6.

[119] John MacArthur, Jr., *MacArthur's New Testament Commentary: 1 Corinthians*, Electronic Edition STEP Files Copyright 1997, Parson's Technology, Chapter 27, "Celebrating the Lord's Supper."

[120] Ignatius, *Letter to the Ephesians*, Chapter 13.

pared and contrasted the landing of the American astronauts on the moon to the landing of our Savior on the Earth. On another Christmas communion we observed the shadow of the Cross in Bethlehem. One year Martin Luther King's birthday fell on a Sunday, and so we celebrated the table around the theme of Two Men with a Dream. Memorial Day has obvious connections to the table as does Independence Day. When we connect the table to these routine events of life, we transform them into platforms from which to exhibit the glories of Jesus.

10. The Spirit's Palpable Presence

Finally, I urge you to prayerfully beseech God to send His Spirit to manifest Himself in a very tangible way during the service. Although we have firmly taken the Zwinglian view of the table in this book, something may also be said for the Calvinistic view, or "spiritual presence." I can attest to many moments around the table when the Spirit of God has manifested His presence with power and conviction. Weeping over sin is not uncommon in this environment. Tears of joy and blessing are also common. People experience moments of awe and wonder as they "get it." When we give the table the prominence God intended, the Spirit is pleased to anoint the gathering by pouring out His love and power in very special ways. I urge you to present yourself as a clean vessel for His anointing, and I exhort you to invite His anointing over the whole proceeding. The first nine things above involve our human effort—they are Paul planting and Apollos watering the seed. Never forget that it is God who gives the increase.[121]

No Pain No Gain

Change is painful. But so is the status quo. Psychologists tell us that we will not decide to change something until the pain of remaining the same is greater than the pain of change. I pray you have decided that the cost of moving your flock towards a new model of the Lord's table is worth any pain you will experience to implement it. Yes, some people will find their routines disturbed. Some might even complain. But I suspect that they will quickly be blessed and encouraged as they spy fresh glimpses of Jesus and His glory. Yes, you will have to exert effort in preparation. You will probably find yourself humbled as you build and work with your team. But again, I don't think it will be very long before the joy of the table will overwhelm you.

---

[121] 1 Cor. 3:6-9. Paul says we are *sunergoi*, God's fellow workers.

Like a woman in labor who quickly forgets the pain of childbirth when she holds her new child, you will find your investment in the table bringing huge returns.

*　*　*　*　*

Appendix 1
Do a Passover Seder with your Family or Church

When I arrived at the conclusion many years ago that it would be good to learn and do the Passover, I began to study it. I studied it in the scriptures, in old scholars such as Alfred Edersheim,[122] and from many strands of modern Jewish Seder traditions. I'm still learning new things about it. One of the things I have learned is that as the Jews migrated to various corners of the earth, they adapted their Passover observance to the setting of their adopted culture. Knowing this, I felt a measure of liberty to adapt the ceremony to my cultural setting as a 20th/21st century American believer in Jesus.

What follows is a Christianized Seder—a Passover/Resurrection Dinner, a composite of ancient and modern traditions. I have removed a few features which unbelieving Jews observe as they continue to look for their Messiah to come as well as those features which evidence pagan syncretizing.[123] This ceremony includes the actual eating of roasted lamb as directed by Moses and performed by Jesus and the disciples. In the years following the destruction of Jerusalem, unbelieving Jews removed the lamb from the Seder and re-placed it with a shank bone displayed on the table. They explain that this is because they lost their ability to sacrifice in the great Temple which was de-stroyed, but it starkly displays their unbelief in Jesus as their Messiah. How-ever, despite these modifications, this Seder should be recognizable to any Jewish person who has ever participated in the Passover.

As you move through its various elements, think about it on several levels. First, notice how much involves *doing*. Then notice how the various *senses* are engaged and stimulated and how the *emotions* are stirred. Notice how *it's all about Jesus*. Notice how the teaching and memory-making is being accom-plished through redemptive *analogies*. And think about how you might find a place in your ministry *to do it* with your people.

---

[122] As a completed Jew who was trained as a scholastic rabbi before meeting Jesus as his Messiah, Edersheim provides unparalleled insights into the background sur-rounding the gospel story. His *The Life and Times of Jesus the Messiah* remains an unri-valed classic. I heartily recommend studying his accounts of the Passover Jesus took with His disciples in the Upper Room.

[123] E.g. leaving a seat vacant for Elijah and the boiled egg which hints of paganism.

A Passover/Resurrection Dinner

The Setting

As you enter the room which has been made ready for the Passover, you are immediately aware that a very special event is about to take place. The savory aroma of roasting lamb instantly reminds you that you came hungry for this special dinner. Exceptional effort has been invested by the cooks to prepare a wonderful meal. The long table covered with the gleaming white tablecloth commands center stage. It is festively set with the finest dinnerware and goblets which are only brought out on very special occasions. In the middle is an elegant floral centerpiece surrounding a fleecy little lamb, and on both sides are two tall, slender candles rising prominently above the whole scene. Several unusual items are placed around the table—many of them near the place at the end of the table which will soon be occupied by the host of the Seder.

The Festival Begins

The guests all take their assigned places around the expansive table. The whole family has gathered for this dinner, and a few special invited friends are also present. The host stands out from the group because he is robed in a full length white coat. He asks everyone to remain standing at their places. Then he lifts a shofar[124] to his lips and blows several sharp staccato blasts, announcing that "The feast has begun." While everyone remains standing, the hostess lights the candles.

Then the host takes a handful of crumbs from leavened bread and scatters them on the floor near the table. He asks two of the younger children to sweep up all the leavened crumbs, while he carefully searches, with the aid of the light of one of the candles the hostess just lit, for any crumbs they might have missed. He instructs them to carry the leavened bread outside the house and dispose of it there. While they are leaving he announces, "This holy feast must be celebrated only with unleavened bread."

---

[124] The *shofar* (made from the hollowed out horn of a ram, or male sheep) is the traditional Jewish instrument used to signal the start of solemn assemblies among the Israelites since earliest times. See e.g. Lev. 25:9 and Joshua 6:4. If an actual shofar isn't available, a bugle or trumpet will work—or even cupped hands around the mouth to make a pretend trumpet.

Next he asks two children to read from cards he has placed on their plate. They read:

Get rid of the old yeast so that you may be a new unleavened batch—as you really are. For Christ, our Passover lamb, has been sacrificed. Therefore let us keep the Festival, not with the old bread leavened with malice and wickedness, but with the unleavened bread of sincerity and truth (1 Cor. 5:7-8).

So then, whoever eats the bread or drinks the cup of the Lord in an unworthy manner will be guilty of sinning against the body and blood of the Lord. Everyone ought to examine themselves before they eat of the bread and drink from the cup. For those who eat and drink without discerning the body of Christ eat and drink judgment on themselves. That is why many among you are weak and sick, and a number of you have fallen asleep. But if we were more discerning with regard to ourselves, we would not come under such judgment (1 Cor. 11:27-31).

The hostess now reads from Psa. 139:

Search me, God, and know my heart; test me and know my anxious thoughts. See if there is any offensive way in me, and lead me in the way everlasting (Psa. 139:23-24).

Raising his right hand into the air, the host now reads the dedicatory blessing from his Seder-Haggadah booklet: "Blessed are You, Yahweh our God, King of the Universe, for You have sanctified us by Your commandments and commanded us to remove the leaven."[125] Now he invites everyone to quietly search their hearts and ask God to prepare them as clean vessels to receive this special memorial of their Redeemer.

---

[125] The Seder was obviously originally written in Hebrew. Each of the several blessings by the host begins with the wonderful Hebrew phrase *"Baruch Atah Adonai Eloheynu, Melech Ha-olam"* (Blessed are You Yahweh our God, King of the universe). The repetition of this phrase is a vital mnemonic tool in inculcating a proper understanding of who God is.

First Cup: the Cup of Holiness or Separation[126]

Everyone now takes their seat and the hostess begins moving about the table pouring a small amount of wine (or grape juice) into each celebrant's goblet. When she has finished, the host instructs all to raise their cups while he recites the blessing over the first of the four cups of the Passover: "Blessed are You, Yahweh our God, King of the universe, for You have created the fruit of the vine." Then he goes on in his prayer dedicating the ceremony to the glory of Jesus Christ, our Passover Lamb, and to the strengthening of our faith and understanding of His glorious work on the cross. Now he instructs all to drink the first cup.

Hand Washing

At this point the hostess begins to move about the table carrying a bowl of clear water and a towel draped over her arm. Each participant dips his/her fingers into the water and then dries them with the towel. As the washing is going on, the host explains that this is a symbol of the importance of approaching this table with a clean *heart*, reiterating the scripture from 1 Cor. 11, read a few moments before. He may also use this moment to remind them that Jesus intentionally modified this element of the Passover by washing His disciples' feet.[127]

The Bitter Herbs

Now the host begins to explain the context of the first Passover, which was the deplorable slavery of God's people in Egypt. The Passover's message of redemption is necessarily set in the context of bondage, and so he explains

---

[126] Rabbis sometime before the time of Christ added the four cups to the simple ceremony instituted by Moses as recorded in Ex. 12-13. They evidently drew impetus for this addition from the fact that taking a cup of wine had become a significant cultural symbol of sealing a covenant (e.g. in the wedding ceremony). They based the four cups on God's self-revelation in Ex. 6:6-7. They designated a cup to each of the four covenantal declarations in that text: (1) The Cup of Holiness/Separation from "I will bring you out," (2) The Cup of Deliverance from "I will deliver you," (3) The Cup of Redemption from "I will redeem you," and (4) The Cup of Anticipation from "I will take you for My people."

[127] It is interesting to note that Jesus utilized the teaching and memory-making power of this hyper-sensory and emotionally charged moment to dramatically lay down memories that probably never left the conscious minds of His disciples.

that the same is true for us today. Like the ancient Israelites, we also need a Redeemer because we are all slaves to sin. With this he begins passing a plate with sprigs of parsley along with a small bowl of salt water. Each person takes a sprig, dips it into the salt water and then eats it. Hopefully, there is at least one person at the table who recoils at the bitter taste of parsley and makes a little "scene." This provides a platform for the host to ask the children to talk about what this all means. Together they discuss that the bitter herbs remind us of the bitterness of the consequences of sin, and the salt water reminds us of the tears we shed when we are enslaved to sin. Then the host brings the symbolism into the present time by asking the group to share examples of the bitter consequences of sin that they might have seen and/or experienced. This segment concludes with the host reminding the group that no matter how bitter the sin we might have experienced, Jesus is able to redeem us from it all.

Second Cup: the Cup of Plagues or Deliverance

Now the hostess quietly begins to move about the table pouring another small amount of wine/juice into each person's cup. While she does, the host engages the children in the part of the ceremony that was specifically commanded by God through Moses.[128] The youngest child at the table reads from a card, "Why are we doing this, _____?" (host's name). Then an older, more capable child reads from a card that was at his/her place setting: "_____ (host's name), on other nights we eat anything and especially bread made with yeast. But tonight we have only unleavened bread. On other nights we eat vegetables that aren't bitter, but tonight we eat bitter herbs. On other nights, we eat meat boiled, fried or roasted, but tonight we eat only roasted lamb. Why are we doing this?" Then all the kids at the table echo in a loud chorus, "_____ (host's name), why are we doing this?"

The host impishly responds, "I'm glad you asked!" and then proceeds to answer these questions and talk about the story of the first Passover in Egypt. He explains the symbolic meaning of unleavened bread—our commitment to live holy and pure lives. He explains the reason why the lamb had to be roasted—the heat of the oven is like the judgment of God which punished Jesus. He explains why we eat the lamb—eating is symbolic of believing in Him and taking Him into our hearts. He mentions that God used ten plagues to convince Pharaoh to release the Israelites and how it all culminated in the tenth plague. God delivered His people through the blood of an innocent,

---

[128] Ex. 12:24-27

spotless lamb which they publicly displayed on the doorframes of their houses. He explains that God commanded they do this memorial every year in the spring as a tangible reminder of their deliverance.

Now comes one of the fun moments in the Seder: The host animatedly tells the story of the ten plagues. He instructs everyone to take their fork and get ready to tap it on their plate as a sign of their amazement at Pharaoh's stubborn refusal to release the Israelites. He graphically describes each plague with hand gestures and grimaces (the frogs, lice, flies, and locusts provide especially great material for craziness as they imagine these critters all over them and in their houses). He may have the young people scratching at the lice and groping in the darkness. As he finishes telling a synopsis of each plague, the group taps their plates with their fork[129] and shouts, "It should have been enough!"[130] Finally, when they come to the final plague, the host responds, "And it WAS enough. Pharaoh agreed to let them go."

When the plagues have been fully remembered, the host declares: "Praise God for His love and power to deliver us from bondage!" At this point someone reads from a card at his/her place setting the first words of the portion of Psalms traditionally read by Jewish celebrants at all their important festivals—the Hallel (Psa. 113-118):

> Praise the LORD. Praise the LORD, you his servants; praise the name of the LORD. Let the name of the LORD be praised, both now and forevermore. From the rising of the sun to the place where it sets, the name of the LORD is to be praised. The LORD is exalted over all the nations, his glory above the heavens (Psa. 113:1-4).

Now the host asks all to raise their glasses of wine/juice. He raises his chalice—the cup of deliverance—high above his head and offers the blessing over the second cup: "Blessed are You, Yahweh our God, King of the universe, for You have delivered us from the slavery of sin." All join him in drinking the cup.

---

[129] Some traditions include a drop of wine/juice with the tapping of the fork.
[130] Hebrew *Dayenu!*

Matzoh Ceremony[131]

Now the host takes up a special three-compartment cloth napkin called the *matzohtosh*[132] or *Echad*.[133] It is made just large enough to receive three square matzoh crackers (which are about 6"x6"). The name *Echad* is especially pregnant with meaning in view of the cardinal Jewish doctrine of monotheism. He asks the group to help him explain why there are *three* matzoh crackers representing the *one* God. After making sure that the symbolism is clear showing God in three persons, and that the middle cracker pictures the second person of the Trinity, Jesus Christ, he removes the middle matzoh cracker. He holds it up in front of the candle, showing them the holes in it, and then he carefully breaks it in half, and returns half to the Echad/matzohtosh. This broken middle cracker will play a vital part in the transition from Passover to Lord's table. Now he tells the group that just as he pulled the cracker out of the matzohtosh, Jesus had to leave the fellowship of God in heaven and come to the earth to be our Redeemer. He had to be broken and pierced (symbolized by the holes in the matzoh). Then after He died He was buried in the tomb (symbolized by hiding the matzohtosh).

Accordingly, now the host excuses himself from the table and takes the matzohtosh (containing 2 ½ crackers) into another part of the house. He moves about making noise while the children strain to listen where he might have gone. At some point in his travels, he hides the matzohtosh, and then returns.

Dipping the Sop[134]

After he takes his seat again, the host now takes the ½ matzoh that remained and carefully breaks it into enough pieces that everyone at the table can take his/her own. He then passes this plate with the broken matzoh along with another bowl containing the *charoseth*. Each participant takes a piece of matzoh, scoops up a dab of charoseth and eats it. As this is being passed

---

[131] The origin of this part of the ceremony is not clear. Likely, at the time of Christ, a cake of unleavened bread was broken in half at this point before dinner. Part of it was set aside and saved for after dinner. However, the use of the three-pocket *matzohtosh* is likely a later (perhaps middle-ages) addition inserted by believing Jews who acknowledged Jesus as their Messiah. They also inserted the hiding ceremony to dramatize the death and resurrection of Christ.

[132] Lit. *container of the matzoh*

[133] Hebrew for *one* in the great *Shema* of Deut. 6:4.

[134] John 13:26, KJV

from person to person, the host discusses what this means. He explains that the charoseth pictures the daily life of the Jewish slaves in Egypt as they had to make bricks and build structures with bricks (nuts and raisins) and mortar (applesauce). When we take the piece of matzoh and dip it into the charoseth, we are symbolizing that in order for Jesus to become our deliverer from sin's bondage, He too had to enter into the normal affairs of our lives by becoming a man and living His life on this earth among us. He had to partake in our suffering in order to deliver us from it.

The host is careful to point out at this juncture that Jesus identified His betrayer, Judas, as the one sitting immediately next to Him and who "dipped the sop" with Him. In so doing, Jesus was poignantly and lovingly showing that He was willing to share even in the sin of His own betrayer.[135]

One of the participants now reads from a card at his/her place setting Paul's words in Romans 6:

> But thanks be to God that, though you used to be slaves to sin, you have come to obey from your heart the pattern of teaching that has now claimed your allegiance. You have been set free from sin and have become slaves to righteousness (Rom. 6:17-18).

Thus ends the Seder *before* dinner.

Lamb Dinner with All the Trimmings

The ceremony now takes a break. The dinner which has been prepared is brought out and served. Effort is spent in making it a very elegant dinner with exceptionally tasty offerings. Anything can be served in addition to the one requirement, roasted lamb. The only items missing on the menu are any breads or desserts containing leaven. Often a plate of matzoh is available to eat with the meal. This portion of the evening is a special time of fellowship and enjoying each other's company. Occasionally there will be someone in the group who is not particularly fond of lamb. The host seizes upon this teachable moment and points out that there is no substitute for the Lamb of God. This night is the night of the Lamb.

---

[135] Jesus had also washed Judas' feet earlier.

Once everyone has had sufficient time to eat the delicious dinner, the table is cleared. Now the host regathers the attention of the group and points out the critical significance of the words "after supper"[136] in 1 Cor. 11:25 and Luke 22:20. Because of Paul's and Luke's insertion of this phrase, we can, with some certainty, accurately pinpoint the place in the Seder at which Jesus said, "This is My body…. This is My blood."

Aphikomen[137] Ceremony—This is My Body

The kids have been waiting for this moment. The host sends them away from the table to scour the house until they have found the matzohtosh (containing 2 ½ crackers) that was hidden before dinner. Usually there is significant squealing and squabbling as to who actually finds it, but then it is returned to the host who rewards the finder with a special treat. Then he reminds the guests about the meaning of this allegorical death, burial and resurrection. This is a time of rejoicing because the One who died has been resurrected to new life. Often it is accompanied by a song celebrating Jesus' resurrection.

At this point the host removes the middle half-matzoh from the pouch, holds it high before the group, and offers the following blessing, "Thank you, Yahweh our God, King of the Universe, for You gave Your only Son, Jesus, to die as our Passover Lamb and to give His sinless body on the cross for our sins." He then breaks the half-matzoh into sufficient pieces for all to have a part of the broken body of Jesus, and then he passes it around the table. After all have received their bread, he again reminds them that as Jesus did this with His disciples He stunned them with the declaration, "This is my body, which is for you; do this in remembrance of me."[138] All eat the bread.

---

[136] *meta to deipnēsai*, the articular aorist infinitive active of *deipneō*, which is literally "after the dining."

[137] The name *aphikomen* is derived from a Greek word meaning "I came." Evidently Jewish Christians of the early church attached this name to the "bread after supper" as a silent witness of their confidence that the One pictured by this symbol had come. Modern unbelieving Jews call this bread after supper "the dessert bread." It is remarkable that they carry out this matzoh ceremony which bears such clear testimony to Jesus Christ simply in the name of tradition.

[138] 1 Cor. 11:24

Third Cup: the Cup of Blessing or Redemption—This is My Blood

Immediately the hostess rises and begins to pour wine/juice into each person's cup. As she does, the host solemnly points out that this was the moment in the Seder when Jesus transformed the long-understood meaning of redemption via a lamb's blood on the door frame into the ultimate once-for-all redemption that He was about to purchase with His own precious blood. Jesus lifted His cup before those men and declared, "This is my blood of the covenant, which is poured out for many for the forgiveness of sins."[139]

The host asks all to join him in lifting their cups of wine/juice in a united gesture of thanksgiving, and then he recites: "Thank You, Yahweh our God, King of the Universe, for You gave Your only Son, Jesus, to die as our Passover Lamb and to shed His precious blood on the cross for all of our sins." All drink the cup.

Fourth Cup: the Cup of Anticipation

Without delay, the hostess rises once more to begin pouring the fourth cup. While she is moving about the table, the host reads the words of Jesus which He uttered as He drank the third cup with His disciples: "I tell you, I will not drink from this fruit of the vine from now on until that day when I drink it new with you in my Father's kingdom."[140] It seems that He was, in effect, saying, "I want you to use this fourth cup to express your anticipation of being united with Me in glory. The next time I take it with you we will be together again."

At this juncture, some in the group may want to express a word of anticipation of what it will be like to share that cup with Jesus in glory. The emotion of anticipation can be an incredibly effective means of keeping memories of Jesus alive in our minds and hearts. Now the host leads the group in all raising this last cup heavenward as he prays, "Thank You, Yahweh, Our God, King of the Universe, for the bright hope that Jesus will come to be with us,

---

[139] Matt. 26:28

[140] Matt. 26:29. The proximity of this statement to the taking of the communion cup is yet another evidence that the communion cup is indeed the Third cup of Redemption. In Jewish Seder tradition, the fourth Cup of Anticipation follows immediately upon the heels of the third cup. Evidently, Jesus built upon this concept of anticipation, transforming it from anticipating the Messiah's first advent to anticipating His second advent.

and then we will be able to drink this cup with Him in His glorious Kingdom." All drink the cup, and with that, the formal Seder Haggadah has ended.

It's All Over but the Shouting

Now various expressions of joy and merriment begin. In ancient times the Hallel Psalms were joyfully chanted.[141] In modern times there is music and dancing. What is important for our consideration in this study is this: The participants of the Passover are given one more opportunity at the end to "do" the Passover. They are invited to ventilate their feelings of joy and gratitude in community and in a very physical way.

*   *   *   *   *

---

[141] Matt. 26:30

Appendix 2
The Seven Feasts of Israel

	Feast	Old Covenant Meaning	Date	Fulfilled by Jesus	New Covenant Meaning
Spring Feasts	**1. Passover**	Lambs killed and eaten to remember the Exodus	Nisan 14 Evening of first full moon after spring equinox	Friday evening, Jesus breathes His last in the late afternoon	The Lamb of God accomplished our **REDEMPTION**
	2. Unleavened Bread	7 days eating Matzoh	Nisan 14 Next day	Saturday, Jesus lies in tomb	We are saved to live holy lives: **SANCTIFICATION**
	3. Firstfruits	First grain harvest offered	Nisan 15 Next day	Sunday, Jesus rises from grave	We have hope of new life: **ANTICIPATION**
	4. Pentecost	Grain harvest celebrated / Traditional day Moses received law on Mt. Sinai	7 weeks after Passover	Holy Spirit sent	God sends us into the harvest field with power: **COMMISSION**
	**Five Full moons intervene—the time of the summer work, and then comes the harvest**				
Fall Feasts	**5. Trumpets**	Trumpets blown for 10 days of solemn preparation	Begins on new moon (dark) near autumnal equinox		Christ will return for us at the sound of a trumpet: **CONSUMMATION**
	6. Yom Kippur	Day of Atonement	10 days after Trumpets		Final judgment will be accomplished: **EXAMINATION**
	7. Booths	Living in booths to celebrate God's grace and provision	Full moon 15 days after Trumpets (7th full moon since Passover)		We begin to dwell with God for eternity: **EXALTATION**

The Beautiful Hands of Jesus

A Sample Multi-Sensory Communion Service
by Ron Kingham

The Setting

The chairs in the auditorium are placed in a semi-circle with the communion table at the center. The house lights are lowered, and a spotlight is trained on the table which is set very simply with the communion elements.[142] A single candle flickers next to them. The table serves as the pulpit so the attention of the audience is always focused on the elements. On the screen behind the table, a PowerPoint slide depicts a close-up of Jesus holding up the bread at the Last Supper with the Title: The Beautiful Hands of Jesus. Musicians are stationed in readiness to play and/or sing when it is appropriate.

A Window to See and Remember Jesus

Would you like to strengthen your love relationship with Jesus? Well, that's just what I'd like to help you do today! Let me remind you that Jesus only left us one place to come and remember Him. It's right here. So, for the next few moments, I'd like you to think of this table and this moment as a window through which you are gazing at your Beloved, Jesus, the One who made you and the One who redeemed you. My prayer is that as you leave here today, you will:

(1) Be touched freshly by how wonderful Jesus is as you see Him from the vantage point of His beautiful hands, and

(2) Decide to offer your hands to Him to serve others in His name.

The Amazing Creation of our own Hands

Let's begin by talking about our own hands:

---

[142] I prefer to have a whole loaf of bread on the table, even if trays of broken bread will be passed to the participants. There is a great deal of iconic memory-making power in seeing the bread broken.

Let me show you some slides of the human hand. (*Show various pictures of hands—baby hands, hands crafting pottery, etc.*) Psalm 139 says God knitted us together in our mothers' wombs. Accordingly, we are "fearfully and wonderfully made." One of the most fantastic things God creates is our hands. They are one of the most amazing inventions in the entire universe. We use these incredibly versatile tools more than any other part of our bodies.

Science hasn't even come close to designing a machine which can work like our hands. Hold up your hands and look at them.

The thumb opposes the fingers so you can grasp things with great strength. Sir Isaac Newton said, "In the absence of any other proof, the thumb alone would convince me of God's existence."[143] The nails are expendable and enable you to pick up very small items. Your fingers are equipped with a great concentration of sensory nerves so you are able to discern very subtle qualities of texture and temperature. They enable you to write, type, play musical instruments, knit, build, hammer, pry, hug, pitch a baseball… etc. They enable you to add a visual gesture to enhance your verbal communication.

If you've ever lost the use of one of your hands, you know how brilliant it is that God created two hands. For example, have you ever tried to put on your clothes with only one hand?

A Metaphor for Doing Things—Especially God's Great Works

Because our hands are so capable, we have come to associate them with doing things. We say, "Let me give you a hand." The Bible also does this. And it associates God's supernatural work with His hands. The Psalmist says, "In the beginning you laid the foundations of the earth, and the heavens are the work of your hands" (Psa. 102:25). We know from John 1:3 and Col. 1:16 that Jesus was the agent of the God-head who performed the actual work of creation. (*Show slide of planet earth.*) As you look at your hands say with me, "Jesus, You are amazing for creating my remarkable hands!" You may put your hands down.

Now the Bible goes on to say that the One who made our hands in His own image, then took human flesh upon Himself and lived out His life on this earth using His human hands to do His divine work of redemption. (*Put this phrase on the screen: Jesus used His human hands to do His divine work of redemption.*)

---

[143] *Human Nature : An Interdisciplinary Biosocial Perspective*, Vol. 1, Issues 7-12 (1978), p. 47

The Beautiful Hands of Jesus—Seen Through Music

I'd like us to look at this today from two vantage points, first musically and then from the scriptures. First, I'd like you to listen to a wonderful gospel song sung by a man with one of the deepest bass voices God ever created, George Younce. His voice will capture your heart. Listen carefully to the words, because they lead us right to where we're going as we remember Jesus today at this table. As you look at the pictures, notice the hands.

PLAY "The Hand."[144] *Use PowerPoint slides to display the words and illustrate some of the scenes depicted in the song.*

The Beautiful Hands of Jesus—Seen Through Scripture

Now let's do a brief New Testament survey of some of the wonderful things the Bible reveals about the beautiful hands of Jesus. As you take in each picture, allow your eyes to zoom in on His hands.

Illustrate each point below with PowerPoint slides depicting each story[145] *and the scripture which accompanies it.*

1. His hands made items of quality in His carpenter's shop. Tradition tells us that Jesus had a reputation for making excellent ox yokes. His skilled hands carefully crafted "easy" yokes, i.e. yokes which fit well and didn't chafe while the animal was pulling a heavy load.

   Application: As you peer through the window of this table right now (*gesture towards table*), see the hands of Jesus crafting a yoke just for you and your specific load. Hear Him say: "Take My yoke upon you… for My yoke is easy. I will help you with your load." *Pray*: "Father, help us all to trust Jesus with our load."

2. His hands displayed His great miracle-working power. The gospels record the astonishment of the crowds who gathered around Jesus: "Whence hath this man these things? and what wisdom is this which is given unto him, that even such mighty works are wrought by his hands?" (Mark 6:2, KJV).

---

[144] *The Hand*, sung by George Younce / Written by Toni Jolene Clay and Ed Miller / © 1998 Yours For A Song Music / BMI / All rights reserved / from the album *When Men Pray* on Daywind Records

[145] Visuals of most Bible stories are available with a simple Google image search.

a. <u>Healing</u>: "At sunset, the people brought to Jesus all who had various kinds of sickness, and laying his hands on each one, he healed them" (Luke 4:40). E.g.:

    <u>The blind</u>: "… Jesus put his hands on the man's eyes. Then his eyes were opened, his sight was restored, and he saw everything clearly" (Mark 8:25).

    <u>Lepers</u>—whom no one would ever touch because they were unclean: "Jesus reached out his hand and touched the man. 'I am willing,' he said. 'Be clean!' Immediately he was cleansed of his leprosy" (Matt. 8:3).

b. <u>Calming the storm</u>: The Biblical text doesn't say so, but extra-biblical tradition records that Jesus raised his almighty hands when He said, "'…Quiet! Be still!.' Then the wind died down and it was completely calm" (Mark 4:39).

c. <u>Raising the dead</u>: With His life-giving hands, Jesus resurrected the lifeless body of the daughter of the synagogue official: "…[H]e went in and took the girl by the hand, and she got up" (Matt. 9:25).

d. <u>Breaking five loaves of bread and two fish to feed more than five thousand people</u> (John 6:5-13).

    <u>Application</u>: As you peer through the window of this table right now, see the miracle-working hands of Jesus reaching out to you. Hear Him say, "My hands have the power to help you, no matter what your need!"

3. <u>His hands poured out His tender love and compassion.</u>

a. <u>Taking up children into His arms of love</u>: "People were bringing little children to Jesus for him to place his hands on them…. And he took the children in his arms, placed his hands on them and blessed them" (Mark 10:13-16).

b. <u>Lifting the sinking Peter whose faith had wavered</u>: "But when he saw the wind, he was afraid and, beginning to sink, cried out, 'Lord, save me!' Immediately Jesus reached out his hand and caught him…" (Matt. 14:30-31).

c. <u>Holding His precious sheep tightly</u>: "I give them eternal life, and they shall never perish; no one will snatch them out of my hand" (John 10:28).

d. <u>Loving His own</u>: "And he stretched forth his hand toward his disciples, and said, 'Behold my mother and my brethren!'" (Matt. 12:49, KJV).

> <u>Application</u>: As you peer through the window of this table right now, allow the hands of Jesus to embrace you and remind you that He loves you deeply.

4. <u>His hands—especially His right hand—symbolize His power and authority over mankind</u>. Throughout the Bible, the right hand signifies authority and power. The remnants of this custom survive today when we take oaths while raising our right hands. Jesus is the judge. John's revelation pictures Him holding seven stars (church leaders) in His right hand (Rev. 1:16). John 3:35 says, "The Father loves the Son and has placed everything in his hands." Jesus gave us a glimpse of His anger with flagrant sin when the sacred Temple was being desecrated by greedy merchants. His hands became the instrument of judgment: "So he made a whip out of cords, and drove all from the temple courts, both sheep and cattle; he scattered the coins of the money changers and overturned their tables" (John 2:15). Peter declared: "He commanded us to preach to the people and to testify that he is the one whom God appointed as judge of the living and the dead" (Acts 10:42).

> <u>Application</u>: As you peer through the window of this table right now and see the hands of Jesus—think soberly. If this were the moment you were ushered into His glorious presence, would you be prepared to give a good account of how you have stewarded His grace in your life?

5. <u>His hands portrayed and dramatized His mission of redemption for you and me—the key reason we are gathered around this table today</u>.

This section should be done rapidly and read with great feeling. The cumulative effect of the quick images and emotional messages will have a powerful impact upon the hearts of the people.

a. He used His hands to wash the disciples' feet in the Upper Room at the start of the Passover on the night before He died. **Beloved, these are the hands of matchless love.**

b. He used His hands to break and pass the bread and bless the cup. **Beloved, these are the hands of matchless love.**

c. His hands were folded in prayer as He agonized in the Garden of Gethsemane, as He grappled with the incredible price He was being asked to pay to redeem the whole sinful human race—including you and me. **Beloved, these are the hands of matchless love.**

d. Though He could have called ten thousand angels, He voluntarily allowed His powerful, miracle-working hands to be tied as He was arrested by the Jewish and Roman authorities. **Beloved, these are the hands of matchless love.**

e. Though He had done nothing worthy of punishment, He voluntarily allowed His powerful, miracle-working hands to be tied as He was mercilessly scourged scores of times across His back with a Roman flagrum. *Have someone backstage crack a whip several times.* **Beloved, these are the hands of matchless love.**

f. Though He had done no sin and was not guilty of any crime, and though He was weak from that brutal beating, His hands gripped the splintery cross with steadfast determination as He made His way toward Golgotha. **Beloved, these are the hands of matchless love.**

g. Those powerful, sinless, holy hands of love allowed the soldiers to drive huge nails into them. *Have someone backstage make the sound of pounding.* **Beloved, these are the hands of matchless love.**

h. Those beautiful, sinless, loving, holy hands screamed in pain when the full weight of His body ripped against the nails as the cross was lifted up. *Have someone backstage scream out in agony.* **Beloved, these are the hands of matchless love.**

i. Those hands which had created the universe were now stiff and cold with rigor mortise when Joseph of Arimathea and Nicodemus gently enfolded them into the burial shroud.

j. Those mighty hands, those beautiful hands of matchless love, were impotent for three days while Jesus lay buried—dead—in that cold tomb.

BUT!! You know the rest of the story, don't you!? Jesus came out of that tomb, alive and well, and in a glorified, resurrected body. And guess what…?

k. Those nail-scarred hands became THE identifying mark which linked His glorified body with the former one. He said to Thomas, "Put your finger here; see my hands…." Then Thomas bowed down in humble worship and declared, "My Lord and my God" (John 20:27-28). This became an awesome fulfillment of Isaiah's prophecy, "See, I have engraved you on the palms of my hands…" (Isa. 49:16).

> Application: As you peer through the window of this table right now, see the nail-scarred hands of your Redeemer in a beautiful glorified body. See the One who willingly paid the awful price of your sin because He loved you more than you will ever comprehend.

6. His hands became the last memory the disciples had of Jesus just before He ascended: "When he had led them out to the vicinity of Bethany, he lifted up his hands and blessed them. While he was blessing them, he left them and was taken up into heaven" (Luke 24:50-51). The apostles went forth boldly preaching about Jesus because they knew they were IN GOOD HANDS!

> Application: We follow in their footsteps. If we will allow the memories of Jesus to ignite our faith, we also will boldly live our lives for Him, knowing that we too are in good hands.

Taking the Communion Together

Continue to display appropriate visuals on the screen throughout the remainder of the service.

Friends, this precious table was given to us by Jesus for the express purpose of remembering Him. In a few moments we will be eating and drinking these sacred elements. As you prepare your heart to receive them, I invite you to reflect upon what we have seen and heard today. Try to wrap your mind around the amazing, beautiful hands of Jesus.

SONG: How Beautiful[146]

> *Have your worship team play and sing it. Put the lyrics up on the screen as the song is being sung.*

---

[146] *How Beautiful*, words and music by Twila Paris, EMI Christian Music Publishing, Hal Leonard Corporation, 1990.

Introduce it: Stanzas one and two speak of the actual physical body of Christ, and stanzas three and four speak of you and me—the body of believers in Christ—who are now the hands and feet of Jesus in His absence. This song powerfully reminds us that since our redemption rests completely in His hands, we can't just contemplate these truths and then walk away saying, "Ho hum." It reminds us: "As He laid down His life, we offer this sacrifice, that we will live just as He died, willing to pay the price…"[147]

<u>Moments of Prayerful Preparation</u>: *While quiet music plays:* The Apostle Paul instructs us to never take this table without first examining ourselves. So I encourage you to invite the Spirit of God to shine His light into your hearts right now. Then appeal to the cleansing blood of Jesus to clean out anything the Spirit shows you is standing between you and Him right now.

<u>Bless (i.e. pray over), Break, and Pass the Bread</u>: *While the bread is being passed:* God marvelously equipped us with our senses. They enable us to see, hear, smell, feel heat and cold, pain, texture, and to orient ourselves in space. It has been my goal today to bring the beautiful hands of Jesus into contact with your senses. As you hold the bread in your hands, your sense of touch is connecting with THE most significant symbol in the entire world: the picture of the body of Jesus our Redeemer which was broken for our salvation. Now I challenge you to look at it, and then replay some of the images and sounds you've seen and heard today. Do you see His hands outstretched to you in love? Do you see Him placing His loving arms around you and blessing you? What is He saying to you? What do you hear? Now lift it to your nose. That's the smell of crushed and baked grain. Jesus wants that smell to remind you of Him—the One who allowed His body to be crushed for you.

Now, there's one more sense I haven't mentioned yet. It's your ability to taste food as it's going down your throat. God designed this table to culminate in eating the bread and drinking the cup because our sense of taste is our sense of trust. Seeing, hearing, smelling, touching… they are all ways to gather information which we can either take or leave. But taste is different; it symbolizes our faith and willingness to risk and commit. If you've been following Jesus for a while, eating the bread and drinking the cup will take you back to the first time you entrusted yourself to Jesus as your Lord and savior. If it's all just coming together for you for the first time today, this will powerfully dramatize your newly found faith in Him.

---

[147] Twila Paris, *How Beautiful*

134

Listen to the words of the Apostle Paul: "The Lord Jesus, on the night he was betrayed, took bread, and when he had given thanks, he broke it [with His beautiful hands] and said, 'This is my body, which is for you; do this in remembrance of me'" (1 Cor. 11:23-24).

Now place that bread into your mouth and taste it and then swallow it. Join me in praying this prayer: "I believe in You, Jesus. I trust You. I am humbled and grateful for all You have done for me with Your beautiful hands. I have joyfully received Your gift of life. Help me truly remember You. I freely entrust myself for all of eternity into Your good hands."

Bless (i.e. pray over) and Pass the Cup: *While the cup is being passed*: The bread which we have just eaten is a rich symbol of the precious body of Jesus. The cup which is now before us is a powerful picture of the precious blood of Jesus. Throughout the Bible, blood pictures the death of an innocent sacrifice which gave up its life so a guilty sinner could be released from the consequences of their sin. When you think of blood, think of cleansing from sin. God can't just forgive you because He loves you. His holiness requires death. This is why we call the gospel the gospel. It is astonishingly good news! Jesus came to be our substitute and pay the death penalty for our sin.

You hold in your hand a simple cup of grape juice—but it is much more than that. Jesus wants you to see Him reflected in that cup—and especially His cleansing blood. So do the same thing with the cup that you did with the bread. Hold it up before you. What do you see? Do you see blood pouring from His wounds? What do you hear? Do you hear Him saying, "By simply trusting me, you are forgiven of all your sins for all of eternity"? What do you smell? That fragrance of grapes was designed by God to shout: "Not guilty! No condemnation! Absolutely forgiven!"

The bread focuses upon Him—who He is and what He did. The cup focuses on us—who we are and what His death has done for us. The cup is about exuberant joy and freedom. What did you or I ever do to deserve this? Nothing! The cup truly is a celebration of God's grace.

Listen again to the words of the apostle: "In the same way, after supper he took the cup [with His beautiful hands], saying, 'This cup is the new covenant in my blood; do this, whenever you drink it, in remembrance of me'" (1 Cor. 11:25).

Now place that cup to your lips and taste it and then swallow it. As you do, join me in this prayer: "Dear Jesus, thank You for Your willingness to pour out Your precious blood for me. I don't deserve Your grace. Thank You for forgiving me of all my sin. I love You, Lord."

Conclusion

I am told that there is a man who begs on the streets of London who has tattoos on his hands. On the palm of his right hand it says "thank" and on the palm of his left hand it says "you." Each time someone places money in his hands, he responds with gratitude. I think that is exactly what should happen to you and me as we leave this place today—we should have "thank you" tattooed on our hands! Jesus has His work of love permanently tattooed on His hands with scars from the nails. You and I have been touched by His love, and He has cleansed our dirty hands. He has cleansed our hands to transform them into serving hands. Each time we serve others in His name, we are remembering Him.

Stand to your feet. Now look at your hands one more time before we leave today. I encourage you to hold them up to God and quietly dedicate your clean hands to be grateful, serving hands. As you keep your hands held high, let's all sing (a capella) the chorus of Twila Paris' song one more time:

And as He laid down His life,
We offer this sacrifice,
That we will live just as He died,
Willing to pay to the price, willing to pay to the price.
How beautiful, how beautiful, how beautiful is the Body of Christ.

* * * * *

Printed in Great Britain
by Amazon

45424770R00079